The End of Oulipo?

An Attempt to
Exhaust a Movement

The End of Oulipo?

An Attempt to Exhaust a Movement

Lauren Elkin
& Scott Esposito

Winchester, UK
Washington, USA

First published by Zero Books, 2013
Zero Books is an imprint of John Hunt Publishing Ltd., Laurel House, Station Approach,
Alresford, Hants, SO24 9JH, UK
office1@jhpbooks.net
www.johnhuntpublishing.com
www.zero-books.net

For distributor details and how to order please visit the 'Ordering' section on our website.

Text copyright: Lauren Elkin and Scott Esposito 2012

ISBN: 978 1 78099 655 4

A CIP catalogue record for this book is available from the British Library.

Design: Stuart Davies

Printed and bound by CPI Group (UK) Ltd, Croydon, CR0 4YY

We operate a distinctive and ethical publishing philosophy in all
areas of our business, from our global network of authors to
production and worldwide distribution.

CONTENTS

For Beth

and also

For Elissa, Joanna, and Susan

Preface

In November 1960 in Paris, a group of writers came together to pledge fealty to a new kind of literature. Calling themselves the Ouvroir de littérature potentielle potentielle (or Workshop of Potential Literature), the Oulipo would seek out, as co-founder Raymond Queneau put it, "new forms and structures that may be used by writers in any way they see fit." This aim is serviceably vague, allowing for a wide range of understandings as to what, exactly, the Oulipo is and does. No surprise, given the diversity of founding Oulipians: Raymond Queneau (best-known at the time as the author of *Zazie in the Metro*), the chemical engineer and mathematician François Le Lionnais, the 'Pataphysicist Jacques Bens and Marcel Duchamp.

The concept of potential literature is founded on a paradoxical principle: that through the use of a formal constraint the writer's creative energy is liberated. The work which results may be "complete" in itself, but it will also gesture at all the other work that could potentially be generated using that constraint. As Queneau put it so elegantly, "the classical playwright who writes his tragedy observing a certain number of familiar rules is freer than the poet who writes that which comes into his head and who is the slave of other rules of which he is ignorant." In this way, Oulipian literature performs a balancing act between produced and potential work, between what appears on the page and what is suggested beyond it.

The best example of this is Queneau's *Hundred Thousand Billion Poems*. It is comprised of only ten sonnets, but these ten sonnets are printed on perforated paper so that each line of each sonnet can be "liberated" from its original poem and substituted in its corresponding line in one of the other 9 poems. There are therefore 10^2 (100) possible combinations of just the first two lines of the 10 sonnets. This foundational work perfectly captures the Oulipo's aspirations: a great Oulipian work is both a statement of what it knows and a gesture toward something infinitely larger than itself.

In the movement's first "manifesto" co-founder François Le Lionnais implies that it isn't possible to pin down a definition of the Oulipo: there is an "annoying lacuna," he says, in the dictionary under the term "potential literature." Whatever the Oulipo is, and the Oulipo has the potential (of course) to be many things, it will always endeavor "systematically and scientifically" to find new forms for literature. Some Oulipians will make their constraints explicit (Georges Perec and Italo Calvino believed this was crucial), while others will leave them implicit, leaving readers, as Harry Mathews put it, "straining to find out" what constraints are at play (if any). Mathews himself has said that he only occasionally produces Oulipian literature, while, according to Hervé Le Tellier, any work created by a member of the group is Oulipian to some extent.

The skeptical reader would be forgiven for wondering whether such games aren't, after all, a little juvenile. Why write a novel, as Georges Perec did, without the letter *e*? But the Oulipo's game-playing fits into a long French tradition: the avant-garde just loves a game, with its rules of engagement and its unknown outcome. It was only a matter of time before a group made games its entire *raison d'être*. (The Oulipo weren't the first to do so, joining the Situationists and the Lettrists and the 'Pataphysicists in the game mentality of the postwar period.) Here, for example, are Tristan Tzara's instructions in 1920 for how to make a Dada poem:

Take a newspaper.
Take a pair of scissors.
Choose an article as long as you are planning to make your poem.
Cut out the article.

Then cut out each of the words that make up this article and
put them in a bag.

Shake it gently.

Then take out the scraps one after the other in the order in
which they left the bag.

Copy conscientiously.

The poem will be like you.

And here you are a writer, infinitely original and endowed
with a sensibility that is charming though beyond the
understanding of the vulgar.

And here are the Oulipo's directions for how to make a metro
poem:

A metro poem has as many verses as your trip has stations,
minus one.

The first verse is composed in your head between the two
first stations of your trip (counting the station from which
you departed).

It is transcribed onto paper when the train stops at the
second station.

The second verse is composed in your head between the
second and third stations of your trip.

It is transcribed onto paper when the train stops at the third
station. And so forth.

One must not transcribe when the train is in motion.

One must not compose when the train is stopped.

The last verse of the poem is transcribed on the platform of
your last station.

If your trip involves one or more changes of subway lines,
the poem will have two or more stanzas.

Play can be an immensely creative experience; for Nietzsche it
was synonymous with creation itself. But it's important to

emphasize that for the Oulipo play has to be capable of, as Mathews says, "producing valid literary results." Whereas for Dadaists and Surrealists chance was the creative force, for an Oulipian the constraint is not an arbitrary choice but a technique adopted to thoroughly explore—to the point of exhaustion—a subject within its given parameters.

Exhaustion is the necessary corollary to the Oulipian concept of potential. The constraint acts as a rubber band, expanding around the contours of the work as it pursues exhaustion, stretching to its limits; then it's snapped, and the work's potential sails out into the world. The constraint creates an environment in which creation can be helped along. Rather than facing down the blank page, the Oulipian writer can begin with a project.

The Oulipians didn't always invent their constraints—Perec claims to have found evidence of the lipogram (in which a work is created which systematically omits a certain letter) as early as the sixth century. And some Oulipian texts are composed without constraints. But each one is *potentially* constrained in some way. Perec at times had a fraught relationship to constraints, saying that "the system of constraints—and this is important—must be destroyed.... According to Klee, 'genius is the error in the system.'" (Fans of the Oulipo have been trying for decades to figure out if there is an *e* dropped somewhere into *A Void*, either by mistake or left there on purpose.) Perec's sense of battling against self-imposed constraints is important, for it seems to run counter to the general playfulness that is an important part of the Oulipian spirit. It is true that Perec's books are frequently melancholy and full of existential angst, and he often set himself a daunting gauntlet of constraints to navigate, but nevertheless, Perec was ultimately playing *against* his own constraints. Perec's games took his ingenuity outside the realm of pure writing and into the realm of play. For Perec, the great challenge was to find the virtue in the constraint.

4

Early on the Oulipo organized the new forms they might discover into two broad groups: anoulipo and synthoulipo. The goal of anoulipo was, as Le Lionnais put it, "to find possibilities that often exceed those their authors had anticipated," which consisted of research into the literature of the past to find the constraints governing them. On the other hand, through synthoulipo Oulipians invented or discovered new potential texts inside of their constraints. In this way, the Oulipo's ethic was an "open source" one, with the aim of adding continually to the body of knowledge of potential literature. This extended into the group mentality of inclusion rather than exclusion: Queneau was deeply bothered by the Surrealists' careful policing of its own ranks, and he wanted none of that for his new movement. Accordingly, the Oulipo did not prescribe behavior to its members or seek to wall itself off from the rest of literary culture—to the contrary, the group encouraged its members to spread its ideas far and wide and began co-opting authors it admired. Once you were inducted (or co-opted, in Oulipian terms) into the Oulipo, you were a member forever: for your lifetime and beyond.

The Oulipo's ideas sound familiar now, but they were extremely unorthodox when the group was first formed. Begun in great obscurity, its esoteric approach to writing almost guaranteed that it would remain on the margins of literature. Yet, over the years, the strength of the work produced by its members moved the group inexorably into the literary canon. The Oulipo's methods of constraint are now commonly taught in writing programs. Perec and Italo Calvino are virtually deified in their native countries of France and Italy. Queneau, though not as widely known as some of Oulipo's members, is hailed by many as one of the 20th century's great authors and innovators. The Oulipo's books are in print in English by the scores. The group remains a celebrated part of French culture, with regular events and workshops. Two of the Oulipo's titles even appeared in *Le Monde's* 100 Books of the Century, a poll of both critics and the French population at large.

The Oulipo has left its mark on art and literature to a degree that only the most successful movements achieve, and it is still going. Since 2010 no less than ten books have been published in English by Oulipians. (Many more have been published in French, the language in which most of Oulipo's members write.) In recent years, a number of popular journals and magazines, both American and French, have dedicated issues to the group and key members, and scholarly studies have proliferated. In addition to the Oulipo's frequent readings in Paris, its members are read in French newspapers and heard on French radio.

There is no doubt that the Oulipo remains a productive and much-admired literary force on both sides of the Atlantic, but today, as the group enters its sixth decade of existence, its relevance and its future are in question. None of the Oulipian works that have made their way into English in the past decade (with the possible exception of Jacques Roubaud's *"great fire of London"* project) can rival the best work published during the group's staggeringly successful run through the 1960s and 1970s. In fact, in many instances the writing produced now is strikingly derivative of prior Oulipian works. Increasingly, the strongest work in the Oulipian spirit is occurring outside of the group, being done by authors working both consciously and unconsciously within its shadow. Perhaps this was inevitable: embedded in the Oulipo's "open source" ethos is the idea of discovering forms and methods that anyone can use, regardless of membership in the group (though they can always be co-opted sooner or later). It is possible that the group has become too inbred: it is now as concerned with archiving its history, carrying on its traditions, as it is in making new literature. Perhaps it is now the case that writers who wish to make their mark by following the creative spirit of the legendary cadres of Oulipians must do so beyond the group's margins. These questions cut to the core of artistic movements in general, commenting profoundly on where true experimentalism comes from and how it is sustained. Can potential literature outlive its potential? Is the inevitable progression of an avant-garde group from fringe to mainstream? Which aspects of Oulipo have thrived, and which have become co-opted and defused? Where is the Oulipo vulnerable to caricature?

But before we question the Oulipo's future, we should know a little more about its past. Throughout the sixties the group remained a lively (if somewhat marginal) part of Parisian literary culture. In his biography of Georges Perec, the great translator and writer David Bellos characterizes the Oulipo as a "discreet little group." Critic and Oulipo scholar Warren Motte calls the group's first years "voluntary obscurity" in his *Oulipo: A Primer of Potential Literature*. Things picked up in the seventies: 1973 was a key year for the Oulipo, with the publication of *La Littérature potentielle*, an anthology of Oulipian writing that brought the group its first wide exposure. That year also saw the entry of key members Italo Calvino and Harry Mathews (the group's first American). François Le Lionnais also published the second Oulipian manifesto in that year, encouraging the movement to broaden itself into all sectors of culture. Key works of that period include Perec's *A Void* (1969) and *Life A User's Manual* (1978), Mathews' *The Sinking of the Odradek Stadium* (1977) and Calvino's *Invisible Cities* (1972) and *If on a Winter's Night a Traveler* (1979). At that point, some of these productions had become very attractive to a wide reading public, both in their original languages and in translation. And yet, as a movement, the Oulipo remained decidedly below the radar— readers who knew and loved those texts had often never heard of the group. It was around that time that the early members of the Oulipo began to give way to new recruits, a major shift for the group.

Many of the best writers from the founding generation were

already working along Oulipian lines in their writing before they were co-opted by the group. They came to Oulipian writing out of their own interests and were brought into the fold after the fact. Notably, many of them did not aspire to join the group, or even necessarily admire it. Mathews told *The Paris Review* that when he first heard about Perec's e-less novel *A Void*, "I was not intrigued, I was horrified." In contrast to these early writers, who approached the group with some skepticism and much independence, the new recruits were more craft- and career-minded. In the seventies and beyond the Oulipo was slowly becoming less about ludic experimental literature, and more about careerism. As Mathews notes somewhat ruefully in his 2005 novel-cum-memoir, *My Life in CIA* (set in 1973), "at our May meeting, several first-generation Oulipians blamed newer members for taking the group too seriously and spoiling their fun." Writing in 1986, the noted French writer and avant-gardist Noël Arnaud (at that time president of the Oulipo) wrote that the group was "shaken to its foundations by its very success." Painting the Oulipo as over-extended and watered down, he decried the "pedagogical necessities" (workshops, lectures and other responsibilities) that were "dissolving" its personality.

The Oulipian writing that we have seen in the years since then has done little to counter Arnaud's disappointment with the group. As we will discuss in the coming pages, the most significant latter-day Oulipians to be published in English in recent years—Jacques Jouet and Hervé Le Tellier—have not been able to match the seriousness of purpose characteristic of earlier Oulipian work.

Even today, the lion's share of the interest from the group continues to abide in the earlier Oulipians: in unearthed manuscripts from Georges Perec and a corrected translation of the book many consider the Oulipo's highest achievement, *Life A User's Manual*; in an aging, but still-producing Harry Mathews; and in Jacques Roubaud, whose monumental *"great fire of*

London" project is only now making its way into English. Writers doing the most interesting work with Oulipian tropes today—including Edouard Levé, Tom McCarthy, César Aira and Anne Garréta—are either not of the group or from its marginalized female sector, and thus are insulated from the oppressive weight of the group's success.

Nevertheless, were the Oulipo to come to an end tomorrow it could only be regarded as an immense success. After over 50 years of existence it has given the literary world dozens of images, words, games and techniques. Most of all, it has produced classic literature. It has thrived while so many other movements have died out. While we do not believe that the Oulipo is over and done, the dynamism of the 1960s and 1970s seems to have flagged. This book, then, explores several crucial questions: What made the Oulipo great, and what can experimental artists of any kind learn from it? Where is the Oulipo falling short today, and what might change that? And how have the Oulipo's ideas reached their highest expression among contemporary writers?

We offer this book to writers and readers of all stripes. Looking around the decaying landscape of American literature, in which countless graduates of writing programs produce fully competent and easily forgettable books, it is clear that movements like the Oulipo are desperately needed. The resurgence of quality literary criticism on the Internet and in little magazines proves that there is still a fervent and sizable audience for literature that is legitimately new and interesting. But US writers are failing to provide it. Increasingly, the most interesting works being produced in English are translations of novels from other countries. Movements like the Oulipo could do much good for American writing, to say nothing of what they might do for France and other national powerhouses of literature. Just as Oulipo's ideas disseminated around the globe to inspire writers near and far, so could the influence of new movements, particularly in a Web-savvy world. We endeavor here to explain the Oulipo in order to give answers to the curious, to offer insight for those already in the know and to provide a point of access for writers who would like to be inspired by the group. A love of literature is a lifelong project of constant exploration—we hope to add a few new routes to our readers' maps.

S.E. & L.E.

Acknowledgments

First and foremost, this book would not exist in its current form if not for Gavin James Bower and Tariq Goddard; to them we say *mille mercis*—or as Quencau might put it, a hundred thousand billion *mercis*.

From Scott:

This book would not have been written without the thoughts, inspiration and book recommendations of some excellent people. They are: Barrett Hathcock, Daniel Medin, CJ Evans and Marcello Ballvé. And thank you to Moe's Books in Berkeley for always stocking the essential authors I wanted to read every time I came to buy another book. Those shelves are a treasure to an inquiring mind.

Huge thanks to Martin Riker and Jeremy Davies of the Dalkey Archive Press for helping me discover many of the Oulipo, and for making them available in English. And likewise to Barbara Epler of New Directions for overseeing César Aira's emergence in English.

And most thanks of all to Elizabeth Wadell, for making me see that literature was my path in life and giving me the wherewithal to walk it.

From Lauren:

A number of pepole were crucially helpful to the writing of this book, whether they realized it or not. Thank you to the staff at the British Library; to Inigo Thomas, Mary-Kay Wilmers, Sam Frears and Lucie Campbell for their hospitality; to Deborah Friedell for morale-boosting; to Mel Flashman for suggesting I do something on Hervé Le Tellier; and to Sharmaine and Thomas Lovegrove and the staff of Dialogue Books in Berlin. I am also indebted to Daniel Levin Becker, whose *Many Subtle Channels: In Praise of Potential Literature* (Harvard UP) is an unmatched source of first-hand material on the Oulipo.

Deepest thanks to Elissa Campbell, Susan Barbour and Joanna Walsh, for encouragement and clarity and inspiration; to my parents and sister for that, too; and to Seb Emina, for providing a steady supply of breakfast, puns and happiness.

Part One

Eight Glances Past Georges Perec

By Scott Esposito

Reality

"The Biblical narrator was obliged to write exactly what his belief in the truth of the tradition (or, from the rationalistic standpoint, his interest in the truth of it) demanded of him— in either case, his freedom in creative or representative imagination was severely limited; his activity was perforce reduced to composing an effective version of the pious tradition. What he produced, then, was not primarily oriented toward 'realism' (if he succeeded in being realistic, it was merely a means, not an end); it was oriented toward truth."
—Erich Auerbach, *Mimesis*

"A work of art provides us with symbols whose meaning we shall never finish developing."
—Maurice Merleau-Ponty, *Prose of the World*

"Collage may be seen as the literary form of humility."
—David Bellos, *Georges Perec, A Life in Words*

"My intent is to write the *ars poetica* for a burgeoning group...of artists...who are breaking larger and larger chunks of 'reality' into their work," says David Shields on the first page of *Reality Hunger*. Both exultantly praised and harshly tarred, the book was, if anything, read—read with a passion and a range that bests almost any work of art criticism in memory. Flawed and problematic as it is, *Reality Hunger* represents the closest thing we have to a mass-consumed literary manifesto for our times. It was reviewed almost everywhere, became an immediate bestseller and received ritual bows by several wizened heads. Jonathan Lethem loved it. James Wood gave it a grudging good review in *The New Yorker*. Zadie Smith famously wrestled with it in *Changing My Mind*. Wayne Koestenbaum called it "the book our sick-at-heart moment needs—like a sock in the jaw or an electric jolt in the solar plexus—to wake it up." And Luc Sante wrote in the pages of *The New York Times* that "it urgently and succinctly addresses matters that have been in the air...[that] have relentlessly gathered momentum and have just been waiting for someone to link them together."

The book got enough right, made enough of a splash and received enough attention at least to earn a place in the conversation alongside the great manifestos of bygone days, but it lacked much of the newness that manifestos are supposed to wear like a shiny suit. Shields claims that the group of artists whom his manifesto represents is "burgeoning," but the great majority of the several hundred writers he proceeds to plagiarize in *Reality Hunger* come from past generations, most notably the middle decades of the twentieth century: Alain Robbe-Grillet, V. S. Naipaul, Bob Dylan, Anne Carson, Samuel Beckett, Woody Allen and Thomas Pynchon. While there's nothing wrong with quoting past greats who predicted the artistic movement you claim is now occurring, the sheer number of culturally recognized masters ensures that Shields is more of a consolidator than an innovator. To really be predicting a burgeoning literary movement, something that most of us wouldn't know about until maybe 20 years from now, wouldn't Shields mostly be quoting writers none of us had heard of? In fact, the closer one examines his predictions, the more backward-looking they come to feel.

Look at his core descriptors: "a deliberate unartiness"; "'raw' material, seemingly unprocessed, unfiltered, uncensored and unprofessional"; "openness to accident and serendipity";

"pointillism"; "self-reflexivity"; "self-ethnography"; "a blurring (to the point of invisibility) of any distinction between fiction and nonfiction." Most of these were present at the beginnings of the Modernist movement at the start of the twentieth century, and by the 1960s all of these had become mainstays of innovative art. In fact, they are all salient aspects of at least one great writer Shields neglects to quote even once in his parade of plagiarism: Georges Perec.

Perec, who died much too young in 1982 of lung cancer, is probably the most widely recognized author from the Oulipo literary movement. In 1978 he published what is generally regarded as the greatest Oulipian book ever, *Life A User's Manual*, a capstone to an extraordinary career. His first novel, *Things*, was published just 13 years earlier and is a somewhat satirical story of two part-bourgeois, part-bohemian young French adults who can't decide what to do with their lives. When it was published, it won the Renaudot Prize and became an immediate sensation. In between those books Perec published an impressive amount of worthy works: *A Man Asleep* (1967), *A Void* (1969, a novel without the letter *e*), *Species of Spaces* (1974, essays), and *W, or the Memory of Childhood* (1975). He also wrote a palindrome of over 5,000 words, a novel called *Les Revenentes* that uses words that only have the letter "e" as a vowel (translated by Ian Monk as *The Exeter Text: Jewels, Secrets, Sex*), radio plays, films, a curious short work called *An Attempt at Exhausting a Place in Paris*, and a novel that was left incomplete at the time of his death, *53 Days*.

Perec is without a doubt among the greatest avant-garde writers of the twentieth century, and his group, the Oulipo, is possibly that century's most successful literary movement. It still exists and thrives today, over 50 years after its inception and has spawned numerous classics of world literature. Notably, the group is relentlessly experimental, excessively avant-garde. Just the kind of thing for a forward-looking guy like David Shields, yet, strangely, both Perec and the Oulipo are omitted from Shields's seemingly boundless reading—among the polemicist's honor roll of reality artists we find none of the writers who formed the French literary group Oulipo. Per Shields's slipshod appendix of sources (which he has claimed was purposely slipshod and only included at his publisher's insistence) there is not a single Oulipian quoted in the book.

At a very superficial level it might appear to make sense that Shields excludes these writers from his book: the Oulipo, after all, are generally regarded as formalists *par excellence*, and Shields hungers for reality, not formal gimcrackery. As the story goes, the Oulipo ignore reality in favor of strange new forms that their writing can inhabit. Their very reason for existence is to use seemingly arbitrary rules to force themselves to imagine these forms. They push the very limits of what can be novelistic—not exactly a recipe for *Netherland*, is it? Their mentor and co-founder, Raymond Queneau, wrote novels that were anything but realist, and they followed in his stead by writing, among other things: an elusive book about Marco Polo telling fantastic stories of impossible cities; poetry written according to obscure mathematical principles; a book featuring 60-odd scenes of masturbation; a book dedicated to "the enterprise of destroying my memory" that its own publisher calls "exasperating" and "daunting." In other words, the Oulipo is commonly perceived as a group that did not aspire to add a few flourishes to the massive edifice of mimesis but to erect their own cathedrals to new conceptions of what could be novelistic. It would seem that the one thing that this very ambitious bunch does not aspire to is to depict reality in fiction.

But then look deeper. Look to the largest, most ambitious Oulipian book out there: *Life A User's Manual*. In its purposeful plagiarism it beats Shields to the punch by a good 30 years. It also anticipates Shields's use of a very artificial formal structure to get at reality: although Perec surrounded himself with a barrage of constraints through which he had to maneuver in writing his book, *Life's* key ambition is "to exhaust not the whole world...but a constituted fragment of the world." The constraints were the path to this fragment, and over the course of the 500 pages that it takes to get there Perec brings in more of the external world than all but the most ambitious novels.

Perec was elusive as to just what fragment of the world he was attempting to exhaust, but there are at least two good answers: the 100-room Parisian apartment house in which *Life A User's Manual* takes place, or the book's key adventure: an absurd quest by Bartlebooth, the central character out of a cast of hundreds, to paint 500 watercolors, have them made into puzzles, complete the puzzles, and then return them back to blank paper at the place of their creation. Taken together, the apartment and the quest form the axes of a coordinate plane on which the full glory of *Life A User's Manual* is situated. Perec's biographer, David Bellos explains just what can be found spread across that plane:

> Perec shows that he can tell fairy stories, that he can construct a novel in letters, an adventure narrative, a business saga, a dream sequence, a detective story, a family drama, a sporting history; he demonstrates that he has mastered comic techniques, the creation of pathos, historical reconstruction and many non-narrative forms of writing, from the table of contents to the kitchen recipe, the equipment catalogue and (of course!) the bibliography and index.

The book is omnivorous as only the novel can be, devouring all those forms, and our world along with it. *Life's* index is over 60 pages in length, with entries for items as diverse as Mark Twain, the Indian chief White Horse, the Treaty of Versailles, Siberia, OPEC, the Goethe-Institut, Albert Einstein, Punch the puppet,

Annals of Ear and Larynx Diseases, compositions by Alban Berg, the film *How to Marry a Millionaire* and hundreds more. As Bellos implies above, the book is also filled with the sorts of things not catalogued in indexes: love, heartbreak, sex, drama, revenge, fear, pity, seduction, crime...really, just about every part of life that one might imagine. Surely there will be some aspects of life that *Life* does not treat (it is, after all, not Borges's Library of Babel), but they will be very hard to find.

There's no doubt that *Life A User's Manual* takes an approach to depicting reality that is very different from the standard realist novel, which we have been conditioned to believe is the best and most-preferred way of representing our world. It's a belief that has been abetted by some of the biggest names in literary discourse and has given rise, over the past decade or so, to a particularly robust discussion of just what constitutes the depiction of the real world on the page and how that relates to "realist" and "experimental" writing. Though not without its enlightening aspects, this conversation has generally fallen into a simplistic dichotomy, where realist writing is described as giving us the real world of everyday life, and anything other than realist writing is seen as directing its energies toward a vague something that no one cares to define very well. Writing in *Harper's* in 2005, the experimental author Ben Marcus offered a good summation of the debate and its exasperating stupidity:

Anyone who has not been invited into the realist camp is slurred as being merely experimental, whether or not his or her language is a gambit for producing reality on the page. Calling a writer experimental is now the equivalent of saying his work does not matter, is not readable, and is aggressively masturbatory. But why is it an experiment to attempt something artistic? A painter striving for originality is not called experimental. Whether or not originality is a large or small myth, an outsized form of folly or a quaint indulgence, a visual artist is expected at least to gun for it. Without risk you have paintings hanging in the lobby of a Holiday Inn. But a writer with ambition now is called "postmodern" or "experimental," and not without condescension. Traverses away from the inscribed literary style—even when they amount to freefalls down the mountainside—are either looked at snidely or entirely ignored, unless the work is traditional at heart but with enough surface flourishes and stylistic tics to allow a false show of originality, so that critics can dispense phrases like "radically innovative" and "a bold new voice," when the only thing new is the writer's DNA.

Marcus does an able job of making the dichotomy between realist and experimental books spearheaded by Jonathan Franzen (whom he argues with in the essay) look foolish, but the problem with this well-intentioned, enjoyable, and frequently insightful piece is that it never quite tells us what's so good about "experimental" writing. Yes, writers *should* be gunning for it, like their painterly cousins, but why? To what end? On this Marcus is silent. It's a pity. Toward the end of the piece he makes a gesture toward answers, briefly quoting everyone's favorite "difficult" writer, Thomas Bernhard, and enthusing about how much he loves being exhausted by his "menacing" and "brutally controlling" novel *Correction*. (Challenging literature would surely get more readers if its erstwhile advocates stopped attempting to praise it by making it sound like a form of sadomasochism.) He only would have needed a few words more to make the case for the value of that gloriously grotesque work: *Correction* does what all good literature attempts, it embodies something "real" about the human experience. This, so far as I can tell, is what James Wood appreciates about good literature, no matter what form it takes, and is perhaps why he is frequently perceived as a defender of the conventional novel. I regard his 2008 book *How Fiction Works* as an attempt to promulgate this view, plus an attempt to "correct the record" in the public perception of his tastes. In correspondence he explained his preference for texts that have no aspirations to the kind of "realism" that was practiced by Emile Zola and George Eliot, his belief that these books are often much more capable of representing the real world as we experience it:

> I see my task, then, as trying to explain how texts feel "real" (how they move us, stimulate us in the world, how they refer to the real, the human, what Henry James called "the present palpable-intimate") without needing to be formally "realistic." For instance, in "Endgame," you will remember that the old parents, Nag and Nell, are on stage, buried in bins. There is a moving moment when Nag, having chatted earlier to his wife, raps on the lid of Nell's bin. There is no reply. We infer from the silence that she is dead. There is nothing obviously "realistic" about this, and yet there is something real, even verisimilitudinous, about it. It is certainly the present palpable-intimate. We instantly feel a small loss: oh, she's dead. It's difficult to explain the human and aesthetic power of such moments, and, as I can tell, this desire to talk about "the real" or "the human" in my reviews constantly exposes one to the charge of being a fogeyish defender of "realism." But I am no such defender of realism, and don't wish to be.

Georges Perec pursued what Wood here calls "the human," though only a few of his works of fiction could be construed as "realistic." As such, he makes a perfect embodiment of the line drawn from Shields to Marcus to Wood. His early novel *Things*, for instance, has come to be regarded as a classic depiction of sixties counterculture in France, despite having little discernable plot and being written in the challenging first-person plural. Similarly, his novel *W, or the Memory of Childhood* is a bracing exploration of his loss of both parents to World War II, though it is made by way of elaborate descriptions of the sport rituals that occur on a fictitious island off the coast of Chile. What these novels remind us of is the commonplace and oft-forgot truth that all art—even so-called realist literature—rarely displays on its surface what it is actually about. Certainly Perec is "about" more than the elaborate word games and formal constraints that he has come to be associated with. His use of collage, plagiarism and non-literary genres to produce reality effects greatly anticipates the kind of writing that David Shields claims is most interesting right now—writing that pursues reality by recycling cultural detritus. And, in fact, Perec informs the work of writers who are currently pushing far beyond the style and aspirations that Shields claims are new in *Reality Hunger*.

Appropriation and recycling are central to Perec's importance to us today because they are how Perec pursued Oulipo's fundamental goal. Oulipo is best construed as an attempt to develop new forms that can withstand the strains of being made novelistic. Oulipo's first manifesto, penned by co-founder François Le Lionnais makes this aspiration clear:

Should humanity lie back and be satisfied to watch new thoughts make ancient verses? We don't believe that it should....

In the research which the Oulipo proposes to undertake, one may distinguish two principal tendencies, oriented respectively toward Analysis and Synthesis. The analytic tendency investigates works from the past in order to find possibilities that often exceed those their authors had anticipated. This, for example, is the case of the cento, which might be reinvigorated, it seems to me, by a few considerations taken from Markov's chain theory.

The synthetic tendency is more ambitious: it constitutes the essential vocation of the Oulipo. It's a question of developing new possibilities unknown to our predecessors. This is the case, for example, of the *Cent Mille Milliards de poèmes* or the Boolian haikus.

In *Life A User's Manual* Perec did both analysis and synthesis. His book devoured pre-existing forms, finding in, for instance, the lowly product brochure "possibilities that often exceed those their authors had anticipated." *Life* also pioneered new forms; most notably the book itself takes on a shape unlike that of any novel before it. In doing so Perec followed the, perhaps prime, modernist commandment to create revolutionary art by making his world new. It is just this purpose that Walter Benjamin claimed a half-century before for photography, an art form that did more than any other to push the classic arts into their modern variants:

> For if it is an economic function of photography to restore to mass consumption, by fashionable adaptation, subjects that had earlier withdrawn themselves from it...it is one of its political functions to renew from within—that is, fashionably—the world as it is....
>
> What we require of the photographer is the ability to give his picture a caption that wrenches it from modish commerce and gives it a revolutionary use value. But we will make this demand most emphatically when we—the writers—take up photography.

First note that final injunction toward writers: take up photography. Now note that there are at least two things Benjamin is asking writers to do beyond that. First, they must place new subjects before the public eye, particularly by thrusting hidden ones to the fore. That is precisely what Perec does with his unending attempts to "exhaust the subject," to see never-before-described facets of everyday things. Secondly, Benjamin tells authors they must learn to appropriate as does a camera's lens. A camera is a tool for taking things out of context: taking a photo is nothing more than selecting a rectangle of the world to be pulled up from its surroundings. *Life A User's Manual* does exactly that with literary quotations and forms, among other things. Perec pulls well-worn subjects from their common surroundings, forcing us to look at them anew.

With this, we begin to see why Perec did not need realist fiction to depict truths that had heretofore never been depicted in a novel. These methods permitted Perec to, as Benjamin puts it, "renew from within." He found ways to make the everyday seem not-so-everyday. This is just the kind of renewal that Shields hints at in *Reality Hunger*, that I believe Marcus wants his experimental writers to shoot for, that even Wood subtly encourages. Examining Perec, which none of these writers has to my knowledge done in print, can tell us things that these critics have not.

Truthism

The philosopher Maurice Merleau-Ponty observes that "classical painting should be the metamorphosis of the perceived world into a precise and rational universe." This insight is worth lingering over. Merleau-Ponty was a phenomenologist, a philosopher who sought to understand how we experience the world we live in. What exactly are we perceiving when we see sights and hear sounds? How are these sights and sounds formulated by our conscious minds? With these questions in mind, Merleau-Ponty argues that painting that adopts a classical view of things—that is, painting that attempts to portray the world "realistically"—is but one interpretation of our experience, one that makes our world precise and rational. But of course, I would not be alone in arguing that what we experience in day-to-day life more commonly conforms to Picasso's Cubism or Pollock's Abstract Expressionism than classical art. Perec would agree. Early in his career he wrote an article on the artist Paul Klee. Discussing it in his biography of Perec, Bellos reports that the author "came to the conclusion that Klee's paintings had to be rethought as realist works. For what, in the end, was realism? An attempt not simply to represent reality but also to enrich and heighten it, an attempt to make reality denser, and to make it *mean*."

As a writer, Perec too has his own method of assembling the world around him into a personal depiction of experience, his own brand of *realistic* writing. His is a way of looking that is governed by very precise rules, the most fundamental of which is exhaustion. Quite simply, exhaustion is inscribed in everything Georges Perec ever wrote. (An interesting choice for a writer working at the height of capitalist culture.) Bellos has called *Life A User's Manual* a novel that exhausts all forms. Even in his first attempts at literature, Perec created complex formal systems which he then attempted to exhaust. As Bellos recounts, Perec's first attempt at a novel (never published) was called *Gaspard* and was to consist of "4 parts, 16 chapters, 64 'subchapters,' 256 paragraphs. It was this *strict order* that would allow the author to digress without losing his thread." In addition to exhausting structures, Perec also sought to exhaust his own personal experiences: Perec wrote in a letter to his friend Jacques Lederer (quoted by Bellos) that *Gaspard* was to be "the novel of unsonliness: I have suffered so much from being *the son* that my first work can only be the total destruction of all that engendered me." It was to be an exorcism of certain ghosts. And finally, Bellos points out that *Gaspard* was to be a "two-part text" in which one part "undoes" the other. In other words, the book would exhaust itself both in form and in content—that would be the very method and purpose of writing it.

This was far from the only time Perec would write a text that took itself apart, or that was exhausted in the process of creating it. For Perec, novels are written like recipes are followed by chefs. Once each ingredient has been used up, once the whole has been simmered until it has rendered its juices, you are left with nothing other than your book. Thus, for instance, in a work like *An Attempt at Exhausting a Place in Paris*, which is just what its title implies, Perec attempts to write about a single Parisian spot so exhaustively as to push it into the "infraordinary." The principle is also embodied in Perec's 5,000-word palindrome: the very form of it is of a story that arcs like a boomerang's path, first flying out and then coming back to precisely where it started. Here's how Perec described his plan for a project similar to *An Attempt at Exhausting:*

I begin these descriptions over again each year, taking care, thanks to an algorithm...first, to describe each of these places in a different month of the year, second, never to describe the same pair of places in the same month.

This undertaking, not so dissimilar in principle from a "time capsule," will thus last for 12 years, until all the places have been described twelve times.... What I hope for from it, in effect, is nothing other than the record of a threefold experience of aging: of the places themselves, of my memories, and of my writing.

Notice how methodical it is—how each place will use up each of the 12 months of the year over the course of the 12 years, how Perec will make use of each of the 12 months in any given calendar year and so on. He will know that his project is complete because it will simply run out of space within the confines of its rules. The intent is to create a way of looking at these 12 places that will reveal things no one has ever seen in them before. Things that only someone with Perec's history might see.

In exhausting the possibilities created by his constraints, Perec comes to see, and reveal to us, those things about the world that he deems important to represent in his literature. It is these things that he deems the "reality" to which his literature should aspire. Perec's pursuit of exhaustion implies a bold idea: the removal from the author one of the most important decisions: to say when a work has reached its end. The story simply concludes when the method does. Similarly, this method forces Perec to create his plot and characters out of what circumstances contrive to give him. This is a way of construing the world that is no less valid than the order and rationality of classical painting, or of realist literature. This is one of the beauties of Oulipo: it gives writers like Perec the tools to create methods that encompass reality as they understand it. Instead of attempting to fit their work into the realist mold, theirs can create its own principles. More than any other principle, exhaustion is Perec's.

Negation

"I do not know whether I have anything to say, I know that I am saying nothing; I do not know if what I might have to say is unsaid because it is unsayable (the unsayable is not buried inside writing, it is what prompted it in the first place); I know that what I say is blank, is neutral, is a sign, once and for all, of a once-and-for-all annihilation."
—Georges Perec, *W, or the Memory of Childhood*

If *Reality Hunger* represents one strand of literary prognostication that Perec's writing offers a fruitful response to, there is another strand that Perec answers just as well: those gleeful prophets of the novel's death.

In order to tell this story we need to take a step back. Perec's writing was in sync with its times in the sense that it partook in the epic process of cultural commodification occurring over the second half of the twentieth century. Products, beliefs and fashions that once existed on the boundaries of society were resolutely transformed into mass-consumable versions that were bought up by the middle classes. *Things*, Perec's best-selling popularization of the bohemian lifestyle, is one example of how he was part of this process. Another would be *Life A User's Manual*, which transmutes into literary gold hundreds of things that one would have never thought to put in a literary novel beforehand.

One important thing Perec helped commodify was negation. Negation was a huge thing in the 1960s, when Perec began to write. It informed and empowered the groups then fighting against capitalistic culture. In his essay "E Unibus Pluram," David Foster Wallace put forth the argument that the second half of the twentieth century was a time of two great changes: first, the development of this "no" of resistance against capitalistic culture, and, second, the co-opting this "no" of resistance into a catchy sales pitch. Wallace identified the "no" of resistance with irony—long a potent weapon of the oppressed—and then he went on to argue that the appeal of this irony had been taken over by savvy advertisers, who use it to make their products hip. The fiction of irony and ridicule, which he identified with rebellious postmodernists like Thomas Pynchon and Don DeLillo, had been taken over by TV culture. "I'm going to argue that irony and ridicule are entertaining and effective," he says, "and that at the same time they are agents of a great despair and stasis in US culture, and that for aspiring fiction writers they pose especially terrible problems."

Perec was one of those writers who, in part, made literature from the irony and ridicule of consumer society. One, for instance, thinks of his character Anne Breidel from *Life A User's Manual*. Anne scrupulously details the caloric values of everything she eats, but she remains steadfastly overweight. We soon discover why: Perec concludes his description of Anne by having her add her calories with her right hand, while "with her left hand she is gnawing a chicken leg." It is a fitting, if slightly mean-spirited description of the mindset required by fad dieting, as well as an indictment of a society that makes weight such an obsession. Such ironic negation of the middle-class lifestyle is a core value of Perec's work. His best writing—including *Things, A Man Asleep, A Void, W, or the Memory of Childhood*, and *Life A User's Manual*—all similarly ironize consumer society.

Yet there is much more to these books than a critique of mass culture. These are books built around missing pieces, feelings of emptiness, unsolvable quests. The same irony that ridicules Anne's fad diet also gestures toward a heavy, existential sense of void. (Dieting is perhaps the single most widespread, obsessively unsolvable, mass-produced quest of post-capitalist existence.) For instance, in *Things* the protagonists go to Africa to find a meaning to life that they can't in France. In *A Void* the absence of the letter *e* comes to represent the absence of some essential quality in modern life that gives rise to malaise. Reading Perec, one senses an artist self-consciously working on a grand scale to generalize this quality of negation to as many forms as possible—an effort to exhaust negation. Such ambitions are of a piece with the Oulipo manifestos, despite the fact that the manifestos are written with a clear sense of optimism. Aware of the exhaustion of art's old forms, Oulipo strove to find new paths for the novel. Perec's optimism in the face of negation is due in large part to how he fought to make negation itself an engine for innovation.

This is a key difference from writers of our own era: negation has become so thoroughly commodified and distributed throughout society that it is no longer a question to be explored but a default stance, a foreboding and oppressive fact that confronts us at every turn. Negation now lacks the optimism of the striver; instead it finds conviviality with the resignation of the wizened. Let us, for instance, look at a piece of criticism published just last year and written in response to three of the great writers of negation of recent years, Roberto Bolaño, Enrique Vila-Matas, and Thomas Bernhard:

> Literature is a corpse and cold at that. Intuitively we know this to be the case, we sense, suspect, fear, and acknowledge it. The dream has faded, our faith and awe have fled, our belief in Literature has collapsed. Sometime in the 1960s, the great river of Culture, the Literary Tradition, the Canon of Lofty works began to braid and break into a myriad distributaries, turning sluggish on the plains of the cultural delta. In a culture without verticality, Literature survives as a reference primer on the reality effect, or as a minor degree in the newly privatised university....Literature has become a pantomime of itself, and cultural significance has undergone a hyperinflation, its infinitesimal units bought and sold like penny stocks.

The title of this essay is "Nude in Your Hot Tub, Facing the Abyss (A Literary Manifesto After the End of Literature and Manifestos)" and it was published in the literary journal *The White Review*. Its author is Lars Iyer, himself a successful novelist of the negation genre who has been linked to such great negation-ists as Beckett, Kafka and Thomas Bernhard. Iyer continues his ironically delivered lament for the death of literature by telling us that "in the past, each great sentence contained a manifesto and every literary life proposed an unorthodoxy, but now all is Xerox, footnote, playacting. Even originality itself no longer has the ability to surprise us."

We should be highly suspicious when any writer who has gained as much from the institutionalized negative, as Iyer has, tells us that literature has no future. Iyer is a fine writer—I have enjoyed his novels and his contributions to literary discourse—but, to put it plainly, with these statements he runs the risk, as one commenter to my blog put it, of merely projecting his own limitations.

In fact, it is strange to see a writer with Iyer's clearly thorough knowledge of the novel decrying its fragmentation as though this were a liability. In truth, fragmentation always has and always will be part of the novel, and this is to its great advantage. As far back as 1920, the cultural theorist Georg Lukács had declared in *The Theory of the Novel* that the genre's defining characteristic is the very fragmentation that Iyer bemoans. What's more, Lukács concluded that this was a very good thing. He compared the modern world to the ancient, contrasting the novel with the epic, and he concluded that Homer's epics were possible because of the unitary, fully formed world in which they were created. The novel, by contrast, is a product of a hopelessly fragmented world and can only deal with pieces of an incomplete reality. "In the story of the Illiad, which has no beginning and no end, a rounded universe blossoms into all-embracing life," writes Lukács. "The novel is the epic of an age in which the extensive totality of life is no longer directly given, in which the immanence of meaning in life has become a problem, yet which still thinks in totality." The completeness of the Iliad excluded any further development of the epic as a form in Greek culture; the very incompleteness of the novel in our own culture is what ensures that it can continually be rejuvenated by innovative new authors.

Among the modern novels that come closest to Lukács' "rounded universe" with "no beginning and no end" we should count *Finnegans Wake* and *Life A User's Manual*. Both books famously end by pushing us back toward their beginning, implying a circularity. Further, they are books that attempt, like Homer's epics, to account for the entire civilization in which they were created. In his *Western Canon* Harold Bloom sees *Finnegans Wake* as playing a central place in Western literature, that of an all-encompassing whole that might engender a new genre of writing. Referring to our own era as "The Chaotic Age," characterized by insurmountable fragmentation, Bloom declares that "if aesthetic merit were ever again to center the canon, the *Wake*, like Proust's *Search*, would be as close as our chaos could come to the heights of Shakespeare and Dante." Later he recognizes the *Wake* as "a history of the world" and reflecting "a profound desire to play at replacing English with the dialect of the *Wake*." Literary critic and author Gabriel Josipovici explicitly links *Life A User's Manual* with Joyce, while also placing it into an entirely different category than other massive, encyclopedic works of the time, such as those of Pynchon and Mailer:

> When English or American writers conceive of a Major Novel they can only think of it as an Ordinary Novel blown up (think of Burgess, Mailer, Pynchon). *La Vie mode d'emploi* is in quite a different category. It is encyclopaedic as *Ulysses* is encyclopaedic, though in its classic calm it is more reminiscent of earlier encyclopaedic works, such as Dante's *Commedia* or Chaucer's *Canterbury Tales*. This is a large claim to make and I never thought to make it of any book written today.

Bloom, who links Joyce to Shakespeare, and Josipovici, who links Perec to Dante and Chaucer, follow Lukács in construing the forerunners of today's totalizing novels as pre-modern works. Their writing is of a different kind from Pynchon, who writes enormous adventure stories designed to demonstrate the impossibility of narrative. Rather, Perec attempts to encase our fragmented world in forms that hearken back to the beginnings of the modern novel—the *Decameron*, the *Canterbury Tales*—when writers still conceived of simple yet powerful structures for projects that summed up their milieu. Complex as they are, Perec's books lack Pynchon's willful sense of anarchy, his determination to overload our traditional understanding of narrative so much that it breaks. By contrast, Perec is like an ingenious technician discovering novel new molecules; his apparatuses supplement narrative, letting it hold structures far larger and far more labyrinthine that one thought possible.

In claiming that such projects are no longer possible, nor even aspired to, Iyer gives us a laundry list of symptoms that has two core issues: unification and innovation—unification is no longer possible, which means that innovation remains forever stifled. Perec responds to these notions quite handily. Recognizing that the modern world offers no formal unity on which to base a novel, Perec and his fellow Oulipians turned to writing constraints to give their novels unity. The case with *Life* is typical. It contains over 100 substories, dozens of major characters, and an immense array of quotations gleefully plagiarized from the world's great books. What draws it all together are the formal constraints. In its encyclopedic nature and its buttress of constraints, *Life* overcomes Iyer's complaint that literature has become a myriad of competing tributaries with no discernable authority to make order of them—and it is worth noting here that the encyclopedia itself is a fragmentary work organized by a formal constraint, alphabetization.

Perhaps if Iyer accepted my appraisal of *Life*, he would respond by calling it a late masterpiece of a now-lost era. And perhaps he would not be so wrong in that judgment. Of all the massive works of our era, none come to mind that possess the totalizing scope of a *Ulysses* or a *Life A User's Manual*. Perhaps the closest, Roberto Bolaño's *2666*, does not strive to be encyclopedic; quite the opposite, it plunges into the void of the individual, of the author, of outright evil. (Bolaño's shorter and much less single-minded *The Savage Detectives* has a far greater claim to being a total novel, yet even that book seems to exult too much in its purposeful marginalization to aspire to the world.) David Foster Wallace's mammoth book *Infinite Jest* is much the same, choosing to hone its gifts on a few core questions, even if it does convey a rather robust sense of the times in which it was conceived.

But to search for a totalizing book in our own era is to miss a key question: Is such a book really necessary to literature? Cannot the sweep of an author's collected works serve a similar, and better, function, one more in tune with our distributed reality? And isn't searching for a book that sums up our world to mistakenly long for something that was dismissed at the beginning of this essay, the *realist* novel, at the expense of the *truthful* novel? As much as *Life A User's Manual* is a product of its time, Iyer's essay against the future of literature is a product of our time. We live in the era of the institutionalized negative, when the "no" of protest has become simply the "no" of identity. Iyer's "no" points not to the limitations of our own literature but rather to the limitations of the inquiry that he makes. To look for a single work that overcomes the fragmentation of our civilization is to miss the point entirely. It is to ignore the fundamental question, What function is literature to serve today?

The Oulipian who today most energetically rebuts the idea of one gigantic, career-girding mega-work is probably Jacques Jouet. Born in 1947 and a member of the Oulipo since 1983, he has reportedly written over 50 books in genres spanning novels, plays and poetry. They are mostly very short works, although some of them approach 1,000 pages in length. Jouet has also, by reports, written a poem a day since 1992; at the very least we can be certain that in 1998 he published a 1,000-page book of poetry, written in just four years, and has released many subsequent volumes.

Jouet is the originator of what he calls a "metro poem," which is a poem written while riding the Paris subway. Per Jouet's rules, a metro poem has as many lines as there are stops on the trip one makes; the would-be poet thinks up a line in between stops and then furiously scribbles while the train is waiting in the station. Jouet once spent 16 hours in the Paris metro on a route that took him through all 490 Parisian metro stops, creating the supreme maximalist iteration of the genre. Discussing these poems in *Many Subtle Channels*, the American Oulipian Daniel Levin Becker makes these poems sound like the least pleasurable kind of automatic writing: "the time strictures make it less like a Surrealist free-association exercise and more like a suicide-aerobics drill for the parts of your mind that usually make observations into ruminations and ruminations into language." Later Levin Becker quotes Jouet himself on the harried composition of the metro poem: "There is no question of correcting one's composition, beyond the time of composing the verse, which means that the time for premeditation is reduced to a minimum."

Although Levin Becker is circumspect and quite fair-minded in his remarks on Jouet, he does level the criticism that the metro poem sounds somewhat "fishy" and that it breaks from traditional Oulipian form by having the constraint be "unverifiable." (One could just write the poem anywhere and claim that it's a metro poem, which Levin Becker suspects of some of Jouet's lines, arguing they are too long to be scribbled while the subway waits at a station.) Insofar as I have read them in translation, the metro poems appear of little literary value; the quality is so middling that I find it all too believable that Jouet hurriedly jotted them on the train. They have the mealy-mouthed quality of a first draft, the easy satisfaction and facile profundity that tends to characterize jottings.

These shortcomings are also present in the novels of Jouet's that have been made available in English translation, which range from divertingly pleasant to downright awful. Jouet is the author of many, many short novels, and in this his graphomania recalls Belgian Georges Simenon, who lived much of his life in Paris and wrote in French. Simenon was the author of some 400 novels, some of them quite good, and I bring him up here because there is some evidence Jouet courts the comparison. As

Levin Becker relates in *Channels*, Jouet once spent 8 hours writing a novel in public in a tent, allowing passersby to watch his progress on a screen. This brings to mind nothing so much as the apocryphal—yet utterly infamous—account of Simenon writing a novel in a week inside of a glass booth in full Parisian public view. This story so delighted French intellectuals that, years later, several offered eye-witness accounts of this event that never took place.

But if Jouet sees himself as a novelist in the tradition of the great novelists of French literature, the translations offer little textual evidence for it. *Upstaged*, probably the best of the translated novels, is a fun little book of 87 pages about an assailant who incapacitates an actor just before a performance and takes his place on stage. The book is part of Jouet's ongoing, multitudinous *Republic* series, which is his main claim to being the most "political" Oulipian currently writing; in the case of *Upstaged*, the political critique comes from a stand-in, who subtly changes certain lines of the play to make social points. As agitprop, *Upstaged* would stand somewhere in the vicinity of a dare-based social documentary like *Super Size Me* and Garrison Keilor's *Prairie Home Companion*—a fun knock at the ruling order, but hardly revelatory, or memorable. To go back to Simenon—the author of more than a few sharp political novels—his books offer the stiffness and density that make their points stick in one's throat. Simenon could conjure characters that were pitiable, loathsome and truly despondent; by contrast, the individuals in *Upstaged* are scatterable abstractions.

For all its shortcomings, *Upstaged* is high art compared to Jouet's *My Beautiful Bus*, which reads like the worst kind of self-indulgent nonsense. (It is so bad that one must wonder why the normally razor-sharp Dalkey Archive Press chose to publish it in translation; surely Jouet's long backlist holds less offensive quantities.) Early on Jouet confides with seemingly boundless confidence that he "supplied the label 'novel' regretfully" to this

35

book because he is "searching for a new form for narrative." He had better keep looking. Loosely based around Jouet's titular bus and its driver, a purposely flat character known as Basile, the book is full of digressions like the following:

> Puss in Boots is not a cat. He would have four boots if he were a cat. Puss in Boots is the author of an adventure who may spend his entire life giving his language to the narrative cat.
>
> Let's sum it up.
>
> Times are tough and the setting is a mill in the impoverished countryside. The miller dies, leaving behind three children. The eldest and the middle child band together to secure inheritance of the means of production and trade — the mill, and the donkey. But the least fortunate of the three heirs, the youngest, is left to starve day in, day out.
>
> As each day fails to fulfill his desire, he remembers the brewing hunger of the evening before; he's still hungry for the following day, and the day after that, and so on until eternity. Even if he were to skin and eat the only inheritance left in his name, a cat, he would still be hungry. Puss in Boots swings a satchel over his shoulder, puts boots on his feet, and sets off on a hunt. He tricks a rabbit into his trap.

One imagines Jouet feeling pleased with his ingenuity for putting Puss in Boots into his novel as a character, but there is nothing innovative here. This tiresome exercise typifies the "experimentalism" going on in *Bus*, which feels more like a very willful attempt to force innovation than the actual thing. By the evidence of this novel Jouet hasn't found anything good to replace the plot that he's out to destroy.

Levin Becker notes that Jouet is the only working Oulipian to "make his living solely as an author," and this seems right; not only does Jouet provide a steady stream of texts for his adherents to purchase, he also specializes in clever ideas that transport well. Above all, his conceits are simple, beguiling creations that enable his followers to believe that they too can create literature, just like he does. While such a democratization of the literary should be applauded for demystifying literature, opening it up to new audiences, this can be taken too far. One should never lose sight of the line, no matter how ill-defined, between true literature — which requires much dedication, persistence, and struggle — and the merely passable simulacra that any intelligent reader might create. Jouet destroys any semblance of this line. His work shows itself to be more about mechanically filling in the blanks of a clever conceit than about marshaling the necessary perseverance to push said conceit into interesting, new terrain. A more authentic poet might take a metro poem not as an endpoint but as a starting point, a brisk brainstorm that clears the way for the real work of the imagination. Yet Jouet is off to the next poem before the last one has even had a chance to cool.

The only grounds on which the metro poems might be interesting as art is as conceptual art. Levin Becker gives probably the strongest possible reading of them as such: "This has...changed what it means to characterize something, whether a text or a gesture or a person, as *oulipian*... First came thinking about the constraint, then the actual production of texts reflecting that constraint, then the actual production of texts whose constraint is their production." In other words, closing the distance between the text and the constraint has taken the thought out of Oulipo: instead of a constraint that forces you to wrack your brains for words without the letter *e*, the metro poem is more like a video game where you have to jot down line after line before the buzzer sounds. Levin Becker is right to call this a democratization of Oulipian procedure — certainly more people are inclined to try and write a metro poem than to write *A Void* — and he is also right that the poems suggest Oulipian production is just another part of everyday life. The observations, while valid and probably the most that can be wrung from the metro poems, are far from interesting. Such ideas have been in circulation for some time and have no need for Jouet to propagate them. By contrast, in *Notes on Conceptualisms*, Vanessa Place and Robert Fitterman put forward a more interesting direction that Oulipo might take. They argue for a kind of conceptual writing that shuttles back between the micro of language and the macro of structure, creating a tension and instability in the text: "Conceptual writing mediates between the written object (which may or may not be a text) and the meaning of the object by framing the writing as a figural object to be narrated." (Later, in conjunction with the writing of Jacques Roubaud and Christian Bök, we will see some of this promise fulfilled via Oulipian procedure.)

The experimental Argentine author César Aira offers an example of what the fulfillment of Jouet's aspirations might look like. Like Jouet, Aira writes very brief novels and has published many of them. Aira even works within some constraints—he calls them "the continuum" and "the constant flight forward"— both dealing with the fact that he never goes back and revises, instead working within improvisation to keep his texts feeling light and perpetually under construction. This is how he once explained these concepts to me in an interview:

The continuum is an idea, or barely a pretention, a theory. An attempt to put in the story's path, without interruptions, cuts, or jumps, those things that give literature its shape: fiction, the reality that inspires fiction, writing, reading, ideologies, effects, caprices, dreads, concepts; also, the struggle and the resultant work, the production and the product. The corresponding figure is the Möbius strip. I discovered this idea, and was seduced by it, while reading a book by [Gilles] Deleuze on film, where, for instance, talking about the film *Cleopatra*, he breaks in with an analysis of Shakespeare, the

Hollywood studio system, montage, use of color, flashbacks, Roman history, Elizabeth Taylor's divorces, [Joseph] Mankiewicz's cinematography. It became my goal to do something like this in a literary story. But all of this, like all theories, falls under the rubric of intentions, and in literature intentions don't count. More than this: I believe that literature begins to be worthwhile when it exceeds the state of intentions.

The constant flight forward would be the mental attitude of whoever wants to mount the continuum. But I fear that it is less of a theory than an excuse to avoid the hard work of revision, self-critique, et cetera. Writing for me has always been the search for happiness, and so it must be done rapidly to cover the most distance possible and without worries of professional scruples.

Notice Aira's words: "all of this, like all theories, falls under the rubric of intentions, and in literature intentions don't count. More than this: I believe that literature begins to be worthwhile when it exceeds the state of intentions." Notice also Aira's justification for his constant flight forward: "to cover the most distance possible." True to these words, Aira relentlessly combines genres in a very postmodern frenzy of activity, but the books that emerge from this process feel remarkably whole, and they frequently partake in an original lyricism that pays due heed to the *jouissance* of fiction. Reading Aira's novels *Ghosts* and *An Episode in the Life of a Landscape Painter*, it is difficult to believe that he did not go back and revise them, for they are so carefully layered, their central images so elaborately constructed over the course of the novel.

The yield from Aira's experimentation is a distinct, idiosyncratic feeling of lightness that infuses his prose, as well as an openness to juxtaposition that creates unusual metaphors and novelistic structures. The ideas of spontaneity and improvisation are constant tropes in Aira's literature; he has claimed that when he writes in cafes he regularly puts into his fiction whatever he happens to observe, no matter how incongruous to whatever he is writing at the moment. But this is far from the semi-automatic writing of Jouet: a day's work for Aira will occasionally yield a page of writing, and he has stated that he throws away far more novels than he completes after being disappointed with his results. Aira relies on his eccentric method to spur his intellect and harness improvisation, but he does not subsume his creativity to it. Also in contrast to Jouet—fêted as a member of the Oulipo and published by France's most prestigious presses—Aira is constantly at odds with the market, viciously satirizing literary culture and artistic pretension while publishing his books with tiny micropresses on the margins of the Argentine scene. Aira has tipped the sacred cows of Latin American letters and argued passionately for new heroes; his authentically polemical spirit puts the lie to Jouet's critiques from within the mainstream.

It is all but certain that Aira will never write a mega-novel like *Ulysses* or *Life A User's Manual*, but one hardly sees the need for it in his case. The handful of Aira's books to be translated so far range from the Argentine hyperinflation of the 1980s to satires of literary conferences, sci-fi horror movies, Carlos Fuentes, Adam and Eve, cloning, theatrical theory, extra dimensions, 19th-century landscape painters, the paranormal, coming-of-age stories, transgenderism, surrealist automatic writing, Latin American literary cliques, the grandeur of the pampas and the Andes, architectural theory and a real-life incident involving ice cream poisoned with cyanide. Despite the great range in material, all of the books at one point or another profoundly comment on spontaneity and its role in creation—their fixation on this theme is so strong that they can be seen as various points on one career-spanning arc that reveals Aira's general theory of art. This could well be extended to the public image Aira crafts in interviews and his novels, the latter of which often feature him, or some Aira-like doppleganger. His literature is truly suited to our era of chaos and fragmentation, and his persona embodies the life of a writer who eschews mercantile gain and trend-chasing in favor of pursuing his textual vision. Through the redundancy, flexibility and sheer quantity of his messengers, Aira has succeeded in spreading his influence with the force of an avenging angel like *Ulysses*. It is a form of literary influence fit to an age which gave rise to *The Matrix* and flashmobs. What's more, Aira's influence, profound as it already is, continues to grow: just in the last two years he has begun to seriously invade the North American continent, and he has now been loudly praised by the United States' leading organs of literary opinion. As they are often the last to get the news, this seems undeniable proof that he has arrived.

Aira's multitudes bring to mind the *"great fire of London"* series by the Oulipian Jacques Roubaud. Seven books long, the series, or "project" as Roubaud frequently calls it, has seen three of its "branches" appear in English. It is, by a long shot, the most exciting and impressive work by an Oulipian author to be occurring in English at this time. As with Aira, the works are thematically connected but distinct, and they can be read in any order. Taken collectively, they might be imagined to constitute a meganovel similar to *Ulysses* or *In Search of Lost Time*, yet they are not a single novel. They are seven distinct books that Roubaud has grouped for personal and thematic reasons, and as such they once again point toward the fallacy of requiring unity in literature.

Roubaud was the very first writer to be "co-opted" by the Oulipo. In his early writings Roubaud combined math, poetry, and the rules for various games into a rigorous and satisfying form of writing that attracted the attention of Queneau. Levin Becker reports that it is now common for French critics to proclaim Roubaud the greatest living French poet, and he has for years been the unofficial leader of the Oulipo, playfully called the "Oulipope." A professional mathematician who for years supported his literary habit by teaching math, his bio simply reads "Born in 1932. Mathematician."

The *"great fire"* project has the feel of a mathematics textbook in possibly the only way that such a claim could be a statement of praise. The books are broken out into numbered sections, with arrows pointing the reader toward footnote-like "interpolations" and "bifurcations." As with a math textbook, when reading the project one has the feeling that each section builds upon the previous ones in a logical, but subtle and elusive way. The books convey a body of knowledge bit by bit (in this case the "knowledge" is Roubaud's memory), even as they quietly turn the gears of larger structural movements. Roubaud is greatly adept at "speaking" through the macro structures of his books, suggesting feelings and ideas through juxtaposition, narrative gambits that unfold over the course of chapters and an associative logic that plays on the formalism of math.

What most makes the *"great fire"* project rewarding is the sense of a search. Roubaud mysteriously embarked on the project after abandoning his novel *The Great Fire of London* (which itself was suggested to him in a dream), and reading the project conveys the distinct feeling that Roubaud is unsure why he feels compelled to resurrect his lost work. Although he has claimed that the "constraint" he imposed for the project was not to plan any of it in advance, it still feels very Oulipian in the sense that the vastness and unpredictability of memory are corralled by the rigors of a mathematical logic. The books exist within precisely that overlap of freedom and constraint on which the Oulipo has discovered its most worthwhile projects. In a very real sense they *are* Oulipo, just as they are Jacques Roubaud.

Plagiarism

Late in his career, Perec wrote a short story called "The Winter Journey" which Bellos calls "the most haunting (and now most imitated) French short story of [Perec's] era." It involves a litterateur named Vincent who discovers a book called *The Winter Journey*. As he reads it he discovers that the author of this book has plagiarized all the great poets of the modern era—Mallarmé, Rimbaud, Verlaine; their great poems are all there, right inside the book. As he reads, Vincent decides to double-check the book's publication date and is in for a shock: it was published in 1864. It is not the author of *The Winter Journey* who has plagiarized France's great poets but the opposite. Somehow they got their hands on a copy of this lost book and took credit for the author's brilliance. Vincent immediately realizes he must make this truth known, but before he can alert the proper authorities World War II breaks out. In fear for his life he flees, the book is lost, and despite strenuous searches he never finds another copy. He can accrue no evidence that the author ever lived, that another copy exists, or even that he did not imagine the whole thing. With his death the world loses any tangible evidence that the great French poets contained in the book are plagiarists and not geniuses.

Among other things, Perec's haunting story is a sly reference to his own *Life A User's Manual*: that book relentlessly plagiarizes great authors, although Perec is so adept at weaving the plagiarized segments into his own stories that one hardly notices. Moreover, Perec's *Life*, like Shields' *Reality Hunger*, uses plagiarism to help break down the very notion of originality. Both *Life* and "Winter Journey" are reminders that originality is always a matter of cultural context, as well as that genius often consists in recognizing the importance of something previously thought of little value. Like the ocean, culture is always in flux; what was yesterday the insurmountable crest of a mighty fashion is today a placid patch of soft, forgotten style. Modes, themes and plots are lost and rediscovered; imagery is recycled, whether we know it or not. Even precise phrasing cannot be claimed to be wholly original, for who knows what words before ours were written and then lost. If one accepts this view of culture, then one must also accept that creation is not the fount of art. Rather, art, like Duchamp's *Fountain*, lies in seeing the artistic potential of something that already exists and having the wherewithal to make something of it.

"The Winter Journey" reminds us that pulverizing authors who benumb the pens of one era are forgotten in the next, and even those monoliths who remain on the horizon come to be read and interpreted in different ways. As paralyzing an author as Harold Bloom's Shakespeare—said by that critic to dominate every writer in the Western tradition—has inspired, by Bloom's own admission, the supremely different works of *Ulysses*, "Endgame" and *The Interpretation of Dreams*. Surely if even Shakespeare can permit such variety, then the very fragmentation and lack of authority that writers like Iyer claim suffocate our great writers today leave much room for creativity. Even more—such fragmentation can be a source of dynamism, an aspect of our landscape that prevents ossification. Now we are free to make new forms from Homer—as Zachary Mason did in *The Lost Books of the Odyssey*—something even the Greeks could not do. Today our manifestos come in the form of strings of quotations—the newness is not in what is said but in how it is arranged.

So it is with Oulipo. True, that movement does have popular-izers like the Jacques Jouets and Hervé le Telliers of the world, clever, salable quantities that play in the sandbox made by Perec, Queneau and Calvino. But there are other writers, both of the movement and outside of it, who have internalized its lessons and created literature, even movements, of their own. Three writers working in the shadow of both Perec and Oulipo show us how that is being done right now.

Remainder

"Make an effort to exhaust the subject, even if that seems grotesque, or pointless, or stupid. You still haven't looked at anything, you've merely picked out what you've long ago picked out."
—Georges Perec, "The Street"

"We don't want plot, depth or content: we want angles, arcs, and intervals; we want pattern. Structure is content, geometry is everything."
—Tom McCarthy, "Stabbing the Olive," an essay on Jean-Philippe Toussaint

In *Life A User's Manual*, Bartlebooth dies while clutching the last piece to his 439th puzzle, a W-shaped stub that does not fit the X-shaped space that remains. As Bellos notes in his biography of Perec, that puzzle piece is one of "375,000 odd-shaped slivers of experience," that is, one piece out of Bartlebooth's projected 500 puzzles, each made from 750 pieces.

One of the things Perec does continually throughout his career, and never with such supreme power as in *Life*, is codify existence into its constituent parts. Perec once said, "I detest what's called psychology... I prefer books in which characters are described by their actions, their gestures and their surroundings." Elsewhere he declares his ambition "to write every kind of thing that it is possible for a man to write nowadays." These are writerly ambitions that are deeply enmeshed in the tangible; his writing pursues the concrete, the quantifiable. He has no taste for the slippery, nebulous apparatus of thoughts and emotions; for him is the solid stuff of genres, facts, things. Though Perec might have begun his career by wanting to write every last thing, these ambitions were eventually tailored down into the more "modest" (if such grand ambition can be called so) goal for *Life* "to exhaust not the whole world...but a constituted fragment of the world." Perec realized that life will not be exhausted; even just a fragment will be a momentous effort. And so when Bartlebooth lies across his puzzle, dead, clutching that last, unplaceable piece, it is as Bellos claims: "The last chapter of *Life A User's Manual* somehow transforms *W* into a one-letter summary of what remains when all is done."

The unnamable is a concept of central importance to modernism—it very well may be the one commonality between all forms of existential thought—and in our own times we have seen Tom McCarthy take it up from Perec. He tells *The Guardian* that "the task for contemporary literature is to deal with the legacy of modernism," and that is just what he tries to do. Described in brief, the plot of his novel *Remainder* sounds like something Perec might have loved: a man loses an unspecified part of his existence when something (we never learn what) falls from the sky and hits him on the head, throwing him into a brief coma. The compensation for this loss of experience is a monetary award of some several million British pounds, which the man then uses to obsessively recreate experiences he and others have had.

The question behind *Remainder* is the same as behind *Life:* what is left once we've exhausted all the life we have to live, and is it ever possible to grasp it and observe it? The *W* (which is actually the French *double vé,* VV) recurs throughout Perec's works as a sort of occult symbol of the void. This void can in many instances mean something like existential absurdity, or isolation, it is also very closely linked to death and experience. In his strange novel *W, or the Memory of Childhood,* Perec uses *W* as the name of a fictitious, fascistic island off the coast of Tierra del Fuego, which he linked to both his experiences as a child in France during the Second World War (to which he lost both his parents) and to the absolute evil of the Nazi concentration camps. In *A Void,* it is not the letter *W* but the letter *e* that becomes an occult symbol possessed of great power. What we would call a lowercase *e* becomes a death warrant: a group of relatives who have the *e* scratched into their wrists (which of course nobody in the book recognizes as a letter *e*, because the letter *e* doesn't exist in the universe of the book) are implacably hunted down as part of a family curse. It does not take too much imagination to see the *e* deriving in some way from the Star of David that Jews were made to wear so that they could be identified by the Nazis—a symbol of identity that could not be removed and that was one's death warrant. From there it is but a small leap in imagination to making the *e* an emblem of cosmic absurdity, radical doubt, emptiness, the unintelligible.

The remainder in McCarthy's *Remainder* is also very much about a conquest of the void that eventually drills down to death. Like much of Perec's writing, *Remainder* is obsessed with creating and following programs of action. Where the two diverge is in Perec's insistence that each cycle is played out once, grandly, and exhausted in the effort. The item that best represents Perec's work is a meal—it can only be cooked one time, because the ingredients are used up in the process of cooking. Similarly, Bartlebooth can only complete each of his puzzles once, because their value is exhausted in the act of piecing them together. Things are different in *Remainder*. Here the cycles are more akin to feedback loops. The book is about a man who obsessively stages re-creations of events from his life and others—he simply has his "actors" re-create the same events again and again, perpetually. These loops pull tighter and tighter around something he wants to inhabit but can't quite name. Late in the book the incessant replaying of events causes the narrator to finally penetrate the surface of things. He muses, "the walls around her door, the mosaicked floor that emanated from its base, the ceiling—all these seemed to both expand and brighten. I felt myself beginning to drift into them, these surfaces—and to drift once more close to the edges of a trance."

As the narrator makes his re-creations more and more perfect he asks his performers to move slower and slower; as the re-creations become increasingly slowed and extended, he finds himself drifting further into these "surfaces" and plunging into trances with increasing regularity. The trances are like the breakers that prevent circuits from overloading. Something is preventing the narrator from pushing entirely beneath these surfaces; every time he approaches this nirvana of perfectly inhabiting a situation, he short circuits and blacks out. That little sliver of W-shaped reality that Bartlebooth can't fit into his puzzle becomes McCarthy's narrator's tiny fragment of experience that escapes his re-creations. They are the excess, the remainders that cannot be reduced to quantification, the void that Žižek tells us "the series of objects in reality is structured around...if this void becomes visible 'as such,' reality disintegrates." And thus, Bartlebooth dies, McCarthy's narrator passes out.

At one point in *Remainder* the protagonist is asked, "does he, perhaps, consider himself to be some kind of artist?" Surprised by the question, he quickly responds in the negative. It is a striking moment: precisely the same question could be asked of many of Perec's creations (one imagines a blushing Bartlebooth giving the same shocked, somewhat ashamed response when asked if his watercolor puzzles are some kind of performance art). Of course, it is not hard to see the relationship of these endeavors to many kinds of art, and perhaps the only difference between artists and these characters is that the latter never imagine themselves as such. But they are after the same thing: an unmediated brush with reality, a push beyond the frame permitted by—take your pick: language, capitalistic society, the religious concept of God, the exploitation of labor, the Other. Such a brush with the real has long been a gloriously impossible goal of modernism, a pursuit at which it strives to fail.

In Perec and McCarthy, this failure is pursued through

exhaustion—they will get to that last sliver of the real by using up *everything*. Organizing a book around exhaustion is a dramatic departure from ostensibly "realist" works, where the fundamental organizing unit is its protagonist's life. Typically, the one quality in common across that all the various, incongruous things that populate novels is that the protagonist comes across them. But *Life* and *Remainder* are not organized in this way: their organization is the exhaustion of their conceit. This act of exhaustion is an attempt to implicate *everything*, including that last true shard of experience that cannot be touched. *Life* and *Remainder* intuitively understand that the point of life in a post-industrial society is to consume: they demonstrate that no amount of consumption will ever be enough, that there will always be a little bit of consumption forever remaining, synonymous with that chunk of experience that cannot be had. The question they wrestle with is precisely the conundrum that Bartlebooth faces when he holds the W-shaped piece that will not fit into the X-shaped hole: these regimens will always be blind-spotted by a piece that remains.

With startling regularity Perec's and McCarthy's fictions end in death. It is a fitting—perhaps the only—way to end their protagonists' cycles of consumption that push helplessly toward that remainder. By definition, death is the endpoint of all experience of life as we know it; it is something that none of us can ever experience, much less make art about. Thus it is synonymous with those remainders that Perec's and McCarthy's protagonists obsess over, those shards of reality that can be intuited but never quite felt. Marcus Verhagen, a collaborator of McCarthy's in his "International Necronautical Society," which somewhat resembles Oulipo for how it has regularly issued manifestos and statements around the ideas in McCarthy's books and the concept of a "necronaut," characterizes death in precisely these terms: "[Death] generally stands as a cipher for the outer limit of description, for the point at which the code breaks down—a point that is often alive, as McCarthy points out, with secret desires.... It seems that this is what the INS stands for: a horror of finished truths and a compulsive probing of the possibilities and failures of language." In the "Joint Statement on Inauthenticity" from McCarthy's Necronautical Society, it says:

> The Statement declares the death of tragedy in which the lonely hero, in death, is rewarded with authentic being. Instead it calls for the comic, the divided and the repetitive: instead of Oedipus, Wile E. Coyote who, like a true necronaut, "dies almost without noticing," again and again, repeatedly.

The statement goes on to praise the "dividual" over the "individual" and then "the residual, 'a remainder that remains: a shard, a leftover, a trace,' and further to the risidual, a laughable doubling." It ends quite forcefully by declaring, "All cults of authenticity...whether they celebrate it in the guise of transcendence, unity or totality, for aesthetic, religious or political ends, 'should be abandoned.'"

What comes out of these statements is a very clear dichotomy between authenticity, that mundane stuff of life that always surrounds us, and the remainders, those deathly shards of the real that can never really be inhabited. We see McCarthy taking Perec's understanding of the remainder to new places for our times, a fitting answer to his challenge that today's authors must respond to modernism's legacy.

Exhaustion

"When I was young, I thought *Life A User's Manual* would teach me how to live and *Suicide A User's Manual* how to die."
—Edouard Levé, *Autoportrait*

"I re-read the books I love and I love the books I re-read, and

each time it is the same enjoyment, whether I re-read twenty pages, three chapters, or the whole book: an enjoyment of complicity, of collusion, or more especially, and in addition, of having in the end found kin again."
—Georges Perec, *W, or the Memory of Childhood*

If there is one recent French author who most exemplifies Georges Perec's philosophy of exhausting a subject, he might be Edouard Levé. The author of four books, as well as the creator of numerous collections of photography, Levé brought to all his projects a powerful exhaustive verve. He died in 2007, a suicide, but the four works of prose he left behind show a writer working powerfully to surpass the author of *Life A User's Manual*.

Unlike Perec, who generally exhausted things he could observe, Levé chose to exhaust concepts. A good example of this tendency would be his short book *Autoportrait*, which consists of nothing other than sentences that denote facts about himself. It is, quite simply, an attempt to exhaust his idea of himself at a given point in time. Or one might consider his photography book *Amérique*, where he compulsively produces photographs of American cities that share their names with major world cities. In both books the project is clear: follow the idea exhaustively, trusting that what comes will be art. Somehow in this widest of embraces he will catch things that are new. We are not far from the Perec who admonished, "Make an effort to exhaust the subject, even if that seems grotesque, or pointless, or stupid."

Autopotrait is just one paragraph, spread out over 100 pages. It recalls Perec's *Je me souviens*, which, à la Joe Brainard, begins every sentence with the words "Je me souviens" ("I remember"). A representative stretch from *Autoportrait* (which could be any stretch) reads thus:

Seeing Harlem from a train a sentence came into my head: "This is not the promised land." I have neither a hunting permit nor a gun permit. Even though the food is bland and more expensive than at other places, I eat in museum cafeterias, their minimalist décor, their luminosity, and the memory of the art I have just seen make up for their lack of character. I am thirty-nine at the moment I write these words. I have seen a work by Damien Hirst entitled *Armageddon*, made up of millions of flies stuck to a canvas several meters square. I drink more beer abroad than in France. My fingers are thin but strong. I can snap my fingers, but also my toes. Since the age of fifteen I have been the same height but not the same weight.

As does Perec, Levé makes his home within the prosaic in order to show us thing we have never seen before. This tendency is related to his love of surfaces—another commonality with Perec—which is itself related to yet another overlap: both men have no interest in psychology, they simply give the details, leaving it to the reader to decide what lies beneath. And Levé shares with the Perec of *Life A User's Manual* (and *W, or the Memory of Childhood*, among others) a disregard for overarching narratives. *Suicide's* English-language translator, Jan Steyn, commented on these tendencies in an interview with me:

> None of his books, not even *Suicide*, delivers a straight-up narrative with a beginning, middle and end. They are frequently compared to pointillist paintings, but perhaps it would be more useful to compare them to his own photographic series: a sequence of similar but discrete elements that add up to a whole greater than the sum of its parts. *Autoportrait* consists of a long list of facts about the author recounted in no apparent order; the narrator of *Suicide* remembers his friend "at random"; the works in *Oeuvres* [a

numbered list of 533 projects, some of which Levé went on to undertake] could be described in any sequence; the stories in *Journal* are only arranged by which section of the newspaper they would appear in. Each fact, memory, work, or newspaper article is self-contained, but each also helps build a picture of the author, the dead friend, the artist, or the newspaper (and hence the current state of the world).

In *Suicide* Levé speaks of his "stochastic" method, "like picking marbles out of a bag," something even more radically executed in *Autoportrait*. These books explode the most constant feature of the novel, the one thing E. M. Forester in *Aspects of the Novel* claimed all examples of the form must have: narrative. In doing so, they exchange a sense of space as it is lived for one occasionally ascribed to God, or painters. As we bear through these books it is as though we stand before a life in which each moment is depicted in a separate panel, all of which we can see simultaneously. The books' only concession to the traditional novelistic understanding of space is that we must read each word and sentence sequentially, but once the experience has passed on into memory, it lingers more like a painting than a story.

It is as though Levé has absconded as far away from the work as possible, has given up his traditional right to suggest the meanings behind the things he depicts. But in giving up this proximity, Levé snatches the opportunity to push us into rarer sensations. We should not be surprised to see that these are the same things Perec nudges us toward. The place that both authors bring us to is one of continual departures, books and essays that in large part are made up of sentences that could be the origin of other books. As Perec writes in the essay "Space," these origin places "don't exist, and it's because they don't exist that space becomes a question." Earlier in the essay he tells us to "play with space...have yourself photographed holding up the

Leaning Tower of Pisa." The idea is clear, and it transfers to his prose: look for new ways of relating things to one another. You should be playful, counterintuitive; that the relationships may rest on faulty logic does not blanch them of their poetic power, the image that they create can replace logic.

Levé's photographs constantly dramatize this relationship to space. He shows young Parisians in chic attire and lush rooms standing in poses suggestive of a rugby match. What space are they inhabiting: rugby match or hip salon? What correspondence between the two that we should be drawing from the photo? Levé's books make us ask similar questions about space: What is the space in which his books occur? What is the relationship between their parts—how does one "map" a book like *Autoportrait*? In reimagining how space may be used by a novelist, they expand the terrain of what may be considered novelistic. Certainly many of the thousands of thoughts that stream by in *Autoportrait* would be out of place in most novels. I can hardly imagine a differently formed novel that could contain them all and not be swallowed up in boredom, chaos or both. One may make the same observation of *Life A User's Manual:* with what other conceit could a novelist have entwined so many lives so elegantly and so meaningfully? In being the first to strike upon that form Perec left us with a groundbreaking document, and clearly left Levé with inspiration.

It is not that their works lack organizing conceits; it is that said conceits are deep wells of darkness that absorb meaning rather than radiate it. What could it possibly mean that the one thing common to all parts of *A Void's* enormously baroque plot is the absence of the letter *e*? Or, much less mechanically, what can we really know of suicide, the single thing common to all of the events in *Suicide*? The novels inhabit these conceits; they take up residence within their confines, explore the spaces, and reveal their topography. The spaces feel new to us because they are places few authors have gone before and also because Levé and

Perec know them so intuitively.

Experiments

In the work of the Canadian poet and conceptual artist Christian Bök we see another response to Perec. Bök is one of those writers whose work is so clearly Oulipian that one is amazed to learn that he is not actually a member of the group; that he should be seems like such a no-brainer that the fact that he has not yet been co-opted is perhaps evidence of the movement's increasing irrelevance. Bök's first collection of poetry, *Crystallography*, uses the properties of crystals as a basis for the forms of the poems therein. His second book of poetry, *Eunoia*, a winner of the Griffin Prize and a bestseller, is a conscious response to the Oulipo. The book's main conceit is to make poetry from univocal words (words containing just one vowel) aggregating them in each of its five sections, one for each vowel. The book also has exhaustive ambitions: as Bök explains at the end of *Eunoia*, part of the book's system of constraints was to use 98 percent of the available words for each vowel. It reportedly took Bök seven years to write and required five readings of the dictionary.

Reading Bök's statements on innovation in art and literature, he sounds precisely like the kind of person who might join a revolutionary literary movement. In an interview with Stephen Voice, he describes how, as a young poet, he eventually came to the idea of forsaking literature that had already been written for the "potential" variant: "I realized then that, by trying to write emotional anecdotes, I was striving to become the kind of poet that I 'should be' rather than the kind of poet that I 'could be.'" In the same interview Bök also strikes a polemic tone, forcefully declaring that artistic innovation has been co-opted by capitalism:

Postmodern life has utterly recoded the avant-garde demand for radical newness. Innovation in art no longer differs from the kind of manufactured obsolescence that has come to justify advertisements for "improved" products; nevertheless, we have to find a new way to contribute by generating a "surprise" (a term that almost conforms to the cybernetic definition of "information"). The future of poetry may no longer reside in the standard lyricism of emotional anecdotes, but in other exploratory procedures, some of which may seem entirely unpoetic, because they work, not by expressing subjective thoughts, but by exploiting unthinking machines, by colonizing unfamiliar lexicons or by simulating unliterary art forms.

Alas, the manufactured sense of innovation that Bök decries here sounds like the work of an Oulipian writer like Jouet, whose sense of experimentalism only stays within the realm of that which has characterized the literary for years. By contrast, Bök consistently forces himself to push his work into new, uncomfortable terrain—precisely one of the principles that the Oulipo was founded on.

Part of what makes Bök's engagement with the English language feel so new is his ability to detach the very stuff of language—letters, phonemes, even the way text prints on a page—away from the sounds and meanings that we've become so accustomed to associating with them. This is clearly a result of Oulipian procedure. In Coach House's "upgraded" 2009 edition of *Eunoia*, Bök appends to the original text various reworkings of Arthur Rimbaud's famous poem "Voyelles" ("Vowels"), which begins "A noir, E blanc, I rouge, U vert, O bleu." In addition to a standard English translation of the poem, Bök offers "Phonemes," "a homovocalic translation of 'Voyelles,' preserving the original sequence of the vowels." Bök also gives us "Voyelles," which preserves "the original voicing of the sounds," "Vocables," "a perfect anagram of the French sonnet," and "AEIOU," which "literalize[s] the title of 'Voyelles' by excising, from the poem, everything that is not a vowel." These "translations" reveal Bök's concept of language: words are not merely units of meaning; more fundamentally they are physical entities that can be picked up, taken apart, and placed back together in a different way. Bök has said that writing *Eunoia* made him see that each vowel has its own personality, that, to a certain extent, the letters that a word is comprised of determine that word's capacity for meaning. Reading *Eunoia*, this does not sound like mere fancy. The book is one of the few convincing pieces evidence I have seen contrary to Saussure's declaration that the relationship between words and their meaning is strictly random.

To take one example, here one can begin to see how, for Bök, the shape and sight of words are a component of their meaning. This is his poem "W," written to Georges Perec:

It is the V you double, not the U, as if to use
Two valleys in a valise is to savvy the vacuum
Of a vowel at a powwow in between sawteeth.

In the first line Bök plays with the French spelling of the letter *W*—"double vé"—which is in fact more accurate of the letter's derivation than the English "double-u." From there, Bök purposely draws on words that contain "vv," "uu," and "ww," even placing them in progression from v to u to w. Clearly, the appearance of these words and the fact that they contain these repeated letters are meant to convey meaning at a level different from the dictionary definition of the words. There is also Bök's pointed (and pointy) use of *valleys* and *sawteeth*, each containing their own repeated letters. What emerges in these lines is a kind of communication through structure and form, even through spelling. Bök is revealing things that have been sitting there, implicit in the words, but obscured behind their preemptory use as units of sound, carriers of fixed meanings.

This approach to language is, if anything, clearer in Bök's previous collection of poetry, 1994's *Crystallography*. In addition to creating fractals from various letters, the book drawn poetic influence from physical processes involved in the creation of crystals and makes poems from the chemical structure of crystals like amethyst and ruby. Constantly present is a sense of Bök's unceasing attempts to find new ways to derive meaning from the words, giving them an almost occult sense. For instance, from the poem "12":

WORD

$= 23 + 15 + 8 + 4$

$= 60$

$= 4 + 9 + 1 + 13 + 15 + 14 + 4$

$=$ DIAMOND

By giving each letter in *word* and *diamond* a numerical value equivalent to its place in the alphabet, Bök shows that they are "equal" in the sense that they both add up to 60. What makes such games interesting is how these equations fit into the rest of the poem. Bök juxtaposes these lines with the following:

THE REDUCTION

OF ONE

TO

TWO TO

MAKE MILLIONS

The idea of getting two things from one plays off the idea of making "W" = 23, "O" = 15, and so forth. And the paradoxical idea of "reducing" one to two, and then going on to make millions from that parallels the strange transition from *word* to *diamond* via numbers. In these juxtapositions, Bök gives depth to what would otherwise be merely clever ideas. This, and not

Jouet's facile metro poems, is how poetry shifts into conceptual art.

Bök's literature also extends to the realm of the conceptual, a practice in which the Oulipo once innovated but has been lacking for some time. In addition to poetry created from Rubik's cubes (each face is stamped with one word) and a book built from Legos (a remarkable constraint in itself), Bök has created something called The Xenotext Experiment in which a gene of his own construction both contains an English poem ("any style of life / is prim") and has caused an E. coli bacterium to excrete, or "write," its own poem, "the faery is rosy / of glow." In a very real sense, The Xenotext Experiment may well constitute the end of Oulipo, or at least *an* end of Oulipo. It is a writing constraint so specific and so determined by the physical processes surrounding it that it can only have meaning as a process and not as something a bacterial consciousness is trying to say. (The only alternative would be that the E. coli bacterium in fact knew that it was writing something.) Yet the bacterium is still the author in a sense: a different bacterium would have necessitated different language, and the biological processes that arrived at this particular text can be called "intentions."

This is the beauty of conceptual art. It needn't have meaning in a traditional literary sense; it can convey information on more allegorical levels, and it is no coincidence that Bök frequently works on precisely these levels as a poet. Make no mistake: Bök is out to broaden the ways in which we conceive of communication. He is adept at using structure, relationships and constraints to suggest meaning and convey messages, to dig past assumptions so implicit we can no longer see them. Even more, as The Xenotext Experiment demonstrates, Bök is interested in finding new media for conveying language. (In interviews he's quite forthright with the assertion that in decades it will be commonplace to convey messages through genetic code. In fact, Bök has not ruled out the possibility that advanced civilizations have already discovered the benefits of doing so and have given us messages in creatures such as viruses.) As such, Bök harkens back to the early years of Oulipo: recall that the group was founded by mathematicians. Le Lionnais and Queneau were both accomplished in math and used mathematical theory in conjunction with literature, as does Jacques Roubaud. Bök's Xenotext Experiment strikes most as exotic and bizarre, but this is exactly what the Oulipo should be encouraging: in the group's early days surely the idea of working on the intersection of math, Japanese Go, and poetry must have sounded as strange as combining DNA and English does to us now.

Moreover, Bök's experiment is a milestone for constrained writing: it exhausts itself in the process of its own execution. Exhaustion, long a goal of the Oulipo, has become guaranteed in this piece of conceptual poetry. This exactly inverts Oulipo, taking it from a workshop of constraints that can give rise to a panoply of literatures to a steel vise that allows just one form to sit within it. From freedom through constraint to constraint through constraint. As such, The Xenotext Experiment forces a reconsideration of the very idea of Oulipo practice, to say nothing of what it asks us to consider about the form of language and the meaning of letters. Bök has called traditional poetry "opaque" for how it is concerned more with the transmission of a message that with examining how such messages functions. It is these "superficial" aspects of poetry that experiments like Xenotext work on. It's very possible that the poems involved are meaningless, yet the questions raised about language and its structures are profound: In what sense is the "poem" written by the E. coli bacterium automatic writing? Can a writing technique that piggybacks on the processes of biological reproduction truly be said to be "writing"? Or, conversely, does Bök's experiment demonstrate deeper affinities between all writing and biology? Just what are letters if they can be coded not in ink and paper (or ones and zeros) but in DNA? What comparisons can we draw between the English language and the language of genetic material? Regardless of where one comes down on these questions, the key thing is that The Xenotext Experiment forces us into new, often uncomfortable, relationships with the language that we thought we knew so well. It is precisely the kind of juice that today's Oulipo—with its elaborate schemes for mediocre texts, its domesticated Thursday readings of crowd-pleasing stories and literary trivia and its endless excavation of its own archives—is in dire need of. It is, to put it baldly, the kind of energy that once could only have come from Oulipo. Sadly, the movement is now much too concerned with glorifying its past and refereeing its present to conceive of something with this audacity.

Finally, Bök has critiqued Oulipo on political lines, arguing that, for example, "we can easily imagine using a constraint to expose some of the ideological foundations of discourse itself." Levin Becker is right to defend the group against Bök's more stringent attacks with the argument that political inquiries "were never the terms that the Oulipo set for itself." It is true that the Oulipo never set itself up as a political movement and has no obligation to question politics, but Bök's critiques clearly do apply to Oulipians like Jouet who choose to engage political topics. Instead of using constraint to write pedestrian satires of political excess—the kind of disposable literature that will be written regardless of whether constraint is involved—the Oulipo must follow Bök's example and envision books whose political revelations could only come through the use of constraint. This would be to return the Oulipo to its original, revolutionary roots. It is something this group—and any artistic group that attempts to impact a busy, distracted, product-obsessed culture—must keep close touch with if it hopes to be significant.

Perception Is Never Finished

Like many writers before him, Perec left an unfinished manuscript at the time of his death. The book, titled 53 *Days*, is about a writer who disappears under mysterious circumstances, leaving behind an incomplete manuscript. The job posed to the unnamed narrator is twofold: figure out the ending of the book (which leaves off at a cliffhanger moment) and figure out what happened to the author, one Robert Serval.

The plot of 53 *Days* plays out with the narrator on a search, crashing through numerous false bottoms: the search for the missing conclusion to Serval's book takes him through numerous texts, with illumination always just around the corner but endlessly delayed. All this takes place in 53 *Days'* first half, which was mostly complete when Perec died. The book's second half, which Perec left incomplete, begins again with the disappearance of Serval, but this time the unfinished manuscript is found in his car. Per the outline that Perec left for the novel, a series of clues would lead this search not toward Serval but rather in the opposite direction: outside the text, to the conclusion that the author of the book that we are reading is one "GP" — Georges Perec.

At one point, the Perec/narrator makes the realization that "the truth I am after is not *in* the book, but *between* the books." It is a fitting capstone to the career of a writer who always based his literary pursuits in a finer perception of the world around him. Perec showed that books are a powerful way to apprehend aspects of the world that could not be seen otherwise, but the path through his literature would always pull readers toward the external world, as though life itself were that final, essential part of any successful literary creation. So often in Perec, the search that drives a protagonist ultimately leaves off at the boundary of the text, as though the book has been an elaborate prank designed to prepare one for that final glance past the frame of the book and into the real world.

The way that *53 Days* drives through numerous sub-texts to get a reader to the margins of the page is very similar to the structure taken by *The Conversions*, the first novel of Perec's good friend and fellow Oulipian, Harry Mathews. Mathews co-edited the manuscript for *53 Days* with Jacques Roubaud, and one must assume that he felt a twinge of recognition when arranging this work that so closely resembles his own. *The Conversions* is a quest for the solution to a riddle, a kind of shaggy dog tale in which the protagonist is continually made to believe that the next little twist to his saga will reveal the solution. Each chapter of the book converts the riddle that the protagonist is trying to solve into yet another form, from a race between worms to novelistic narrative to letters to a science experiment and so on. Notably, each step of the quest becomes so immersive in its baroque complexity that one constantly loses sight of the overall shape of the pursuit: reading *The Conversions* is a bit like being led through a dark wooded path by a companion who is so chatty about the most esoteric subjects that you entirely lose track of all the forks you've taken, having only your memories of the chatty words to hold on to.

The book ends on one of the most startling images I can remember having been led, stumblingly, toward. In its majestic beauty and metaphorical directness it rises from the book's thicket plot like an enormous, extinct volcano. The narrator, hoping to finally answer his riddle, is sent to a remote island where he discovers a sort of perpetual motion machine. A pendulum that tracks the phases of the moon is kept in motion by generations of fish (I do not think it is a coincidence that they are herring), who themselves are fed and disposed of by an elaborate mechanism. The fish, seemingly, are ignorant of a reality beyond their confines; to them the world in which they are trapped represents the whole of the universe. They are likewise unaware that the motion of their swimming powers a device whose purpose is utterly beyond their understanding.

They are well fed and apparently content enough to not have disrupted the workings of this very fragile system. As we read Mathews' sparse description of this enigmatic construct, the knowledge that his narrator has been pushed toward throughout the novel is revealed: not an answer to a riddle but an awareness of how desires impose limits on our perception. Reading Mathews' melancholy description of the mechanism, one cannot help but feel a little like the imprisoned fish, condemned to spend their lives as an unwilling, unwitting part of a tool constructed long ago by an unknown intelligence to an obscure end. It is perhaps also a metaphor for the lot of the writer, particularly that of the Oulipo writer laboring within a machine of his own construction.

Writers of quality are similar to like Mathews' futile riddler in that they are not content to work within their own boundaries, nor within our own boundaries as a species. They fight to extend perception. It is one of the most important fights a writer can wage, if not the most, for the ability to perceive what cannot be seen by others is what gives an author's work its unique quality. Perec's continual drive through the frame of his creations baits his perception ever farther away from the commonplace. One sees a similar aspect in McCarthy, Levé and Bök, an ambition to take preferred literary enterprises of the twentieth century to places they have not yet been by pushing them through their long-established frames.

Oulipo's most important legacy may very well be its way of imposing things beyond the text onto everything that occurs within it. Perec's elaborate formal structures have the pleasing quality of mathematics; they are problems that can be solved, like geometric proofs, in ways that novelistic questions of plot and character will not admit solutions. Yet, reading Perec one feels an author constantly at pains to rupture these formal systems. His complex combinatorial schemes are metaphors for the needs that impel writers to fill up books with their imaginative creations. Perec simply makes these needs into concrete, fanciful equations that anyone might marvel at—a novel without the letter *e*! They are, like Mathews' moon-tracker, devices for transforming our own inevitable actions into a consequence of mysterious intent. In the movements of the mechanical hands that track the phases of the moon we see but one form of human understanding for an object of limitless inquiry. The potentially infinite conversions that make up Mathews' plot show us others. These devices permit any number of transformations of creative energy. It is in the process of conversion that perception is released, that we are pushed beyond the frame of the text and challenged to see something in our world that we have never before noticed.

So long as there are humans to make it, art will rejuvenate itself at the fountain of human perceptions. This ongoing task will continue to assume new forms as each epoch of human life rambles toward ever more distant horizons. What the Oulipo has given us—and what I believe McCarthy, Levé, Bök and others are taking up in its stead—are ways of contemplating those evanescent structures that lie within the mechanics of perception. Hence, they are tools for pushing perception toward the endpoint it will never reach. It is, ultimately, work that will keep that uniquely omnivorous form known as literature new.

Part Two

Oulipo Lite

by Lauren Elkin

"Between two words in a sentence, there exists an infinity of others."
—Raymond Queneau

In 1986 the Oulipo's second president, Noël Arnaud, was worried about the future of the group. In his "Prolegomena to a Fourth Oulipo Manifesto—or not," Arnaud calls the group's embrace of potential literature both its survival and its downfall: the ouvroir will survive, he writes, as long as it has not exhausted its potential. Exhaustion being one of Georges Perec's favorite Oulipian exercises, you can see the problem: for the Oulipo to survive, there must always be potentially more to do.

In 1986, when Arnaud confided these fears, the Oulipo was in need of direction. It had begun to lose the most dynamic, visionary members of its early period; Perec had died in 1982, co-founder François Le Lionnais in 1984, Luc Etienne in 1984, Italo Calvino in 1985. (The founding lions of the group were already long gone—Queneau in 1976, Marcel Duchamp in 1968, Albert-Marie Schmidt in 1966.) The original group had been somewhat clandestine, even cloistered, and the founders hadn't wanted to court the spotlight by going public; having kept a low profile throughout the 1960s, the Oulipo didn't publish anything as a group until 1973. As the Oulipo became known during the 1980s for its particular brand of ludic literary experimentation, the way forward seemed to be through wit, humor and public performance. But today, as the Oulipo enters its sixth decade of existence, the moment seems opportune to reevaluate if that's the best way for the Oulipo to continue.

Arnaud was concerned that the Oulipo was becoming a victim of its own success, that its numbers were unequal to the demand placed upon them to lecture, lead workshops and make appearances, and that its "personality" was being "dissolved" by the pressure to turn the Oulipo into pedagogy. "It is becoming a 'writers' workshop," he wrote, in an ominous tone. The comparison is apt; the writing produced in a writers' workshop is often inspired by a prompt, just as Oulipian work is inspired by a constraint. Both kinds of writing are generated not by literary inspiration, or by an ineffable flash of genius, but by a concrete task to be fulfilled. As a result, it could easily be said that workshop writing is mechanical and formulaic, and that Oulipian writing is—well—kind of pointless. For better or for worse, formulas and mechanics are at the heart of the writing workshop as well as of Oulipian procedure. What then raises this work above mere mechanics to the level of art? Oulipo, like any good writing produced in a writers' workshop, relies on that extra ineffable something that transcends the mechanism of its creation.

Arnaud was right to worry: today the Oulipo is vulnerable to exhaustion because performance—or rather, self-performance—has become a central part of the Oulipo's activities. There are the weekly performances at the Bibliothèque Nationale de France, the frequent appearances at international literary festivals, the annual summer workshop where amateurs can pay to come and be taught Oulipian technique by actual Oulipians, who are becoming "seasoned performers," working on their stage presence, cultivating a participation-loving audience. But some of the old Oulipian guard are dismayed by this. According to Daniel Levin Becker (the group's youngest member, co-opted in 2009) in his new book *Many Subtle Channels: In Praise of Potential Literature*, the late François Caradec lamented that the group had gone from being a "société de littérature" to a "société de spectacle," producing "Oulipo light," as opposed to—as Jacques

Roubaud puts it—"Oulipo 'ard." Oulipo light plays all the games of Oulipo 'ard, with little of the substance. "A reliable indicator of Oulipo light," Levin Becker writes, "is that a second 'reader' is needed to make certain noises every now and then"— like the time when Marcel Bénabou read a poem which called for Frédéric Forte to ring a bell "at each instance of a word borrowed or adapted from Arabic." Roubaud's work, by contrast, blends poetry and mathematics with a high moral seriousness, though it is not without wit and levity, and is considered by the group both to have laid the solid foundations on which it stands today as well as to point a methodical and engaged way forward.

The crowds that gather at these performances, Levin Becker says, are generally familiar with the basic Oulipian games and would scowl resentfully if a member condescended to explain what a lipogram is (a text composed without the use of a particular letter: Georges Perec's novel *A Void* is written entirely without the letter *e* and is therefore a "lipogram in e"). They play along at guessing games like the chicago (according to Levin Becker, a "guessing game where four sets of words or phrases with similar syntax act as clues for a fifth set that is also the homophonized name of a city"), or a variant of a game called a morale élémentaire in which Oulipians recite a phrase like "dim blaze" or "wan flame" and the audience has to guess which famous work of literature he is referring to (in this, Levin Becker's example, the answer is: "Pale Fire!").

The problem may be that the group is weighed down by its own past; whereas the Oulipo was founded with the twin aims of researching (anoulipism) and producing (synthoulipism) potential literature, today research has won out, and creation takes place in the modes already laid out by earlier generations of Oulipians. The younger generation is hard put to come up with anything new—and they're well aware of this problem. "What's changed since those years is not so much the workshop's relationship to the past as its relationship to *its* past," Levin

68

Becker observes; not one of their public readings goes by "without at least a few texts by someone no longer alive."

The group's most prolific producer of Oulipo light—or Oulipo lite—has to be Hervé Le Tellier. Although he has written an exhaustive scholarly study of the Oulipo, called *Esthétique de l'Oulipo*, Le Tellier's creative work is diverting but, on the whole, philosophically unserious. It lacks the drive to take the world apart in order to better rebuild it that characterizes the work of Perec, or the less well-known Oulipian Anne Garréta. Queneau defined Oulipians as "rats who build the labyrinth from which they plan to escape." But merely to build the maze and escape from it is not sufficient: the Oulipian Harry Mathews has said that the successful Oulipian work "has to be capable of producing valid literary results." Le Tellier sets himself only medium-interesting and often juvenile constraints, and plays it safe in executing them. You get the feeling, reading Levin Becker's description of him, that this is one of the great open secrets of the Oulipo:

[Le Tellier's] books barely conceal a sentimentality both poignant and endearing; in person he has a magnetism that's all brooding humor and sniperlike wit, and you get the sense that for him keeping the room in thrall is second nature, not because it's fun but because it's emotionally necessary. He is forever late, distracted, shabbily put together, despite all of which there is an ineffable seductive quality about him. (He also has this tic where every third blink or so is a veritable flutter of eyelashes, which probably helps a little).

In addition to being the most media-savvy of the Oulipians (he's the one who sends out the most Facebook invites), Le Tellier is also the most frustratingly macho member of the group. In his work, misogyny and the marketplace collide, and the results are bad for the Oulipo. The group may not necessarily condone Le

Tellier's sexism, but they overlook it. What are they going to do? They can't throw him out. Once you're in, you're a member for life.

But why should we take Le Tellier seriously? He's just one member of a group that, while generally acknowledged as an important part of French literary culture, still remains unknown even to well-read people. And yet in 2011 Le Tellier was the most widely-read (living) Oulipian in America, in addition to his ongoing visibility in France as a columnist for Le Monde and a member of the beloved France Culture radio show *Les Papous dans la tête*. He may be the Oulipo's class clown, but surely what a group of people find amusing reveals something crucial about their values.

69 Theses, Notes, and Observations on Why Hervé Le Tellier Matters

1. Le Tellier joined the Oulipo in December 1992, on the strength of his first novel, *The Nostalgia Thief*.
2. He's got a knack for picking up on the procedures invented by other Oulipians.
3. He generated the exercise that would become the book *Oulipo c'est un métier d'homme* ["Oulipo is a man's job"].
4. Here's how that happened: Paul Fournel wrote a story about a professional skier. It began, "My job consists of going down the mountain from top to bottom. To go down it as quickly as possible. This is a man's job."
5. Then Le Tellier wrote his own variation, swapping out "skier" for "seducer": "My art consists of seducing women over the course of an evening. Of seducing them as quickly as possible. This is a man's art."
6. There's something kind of feckless about his will to seduction that makes you want to overlook it. He's just a harmless tombeur, isn't he?
7. Tombeur, n.m. French for a man, usually older, who won't

leave you alone if you're young, pretty and female.

8. He is known within Oulipian circles for being a "notorious wit," which is ironic if you've read his work.

9. 2011 saw four of his books published in English.

10. Other Press kicked things off in February with *Enough About Love* and *The Intervention of a Good Man* (published as an e-book).

11. Dalkey Archive responded in July with *The Sextine Chapel* and *A Thousand Pearls (For a Thousand Pennies)*.

12. Those four books were divided up between two very different publishers: Other Press is known for its dedication to (foreign) literary fiction, while Dalkey Archive is known for its dedication to (foreign) experimental fiction.

13. If you Venn Diagram Le Tellier across those two houses the only thing they'd have in common is his byline.

14. *Enough About Love* would be too conventional for Dalkey, and *The Sextine Chapel* too weird for Other.

15. The only one of the four to be a commercial success was *Enough About Love,* but it was successful enough that Other Press will bring out Le Tellier's most recent novel, *Eléctrico W,* next year.

16. *Enough About Love* is an urbane French book about love and adultery, told in a more or less straightforward chronological narrative, while the Dalkey books are "experimental" works in a fragmented, explicitly Oulipian mode.

17. *Enough About Love's* readers went on and on about its lovable qualities.

18. Lorin Stein called it "awfully cute" in *Harper's.*

19. *The Washington Post* was moved to ask "What could be more romantic than falling in love in Paris?" and could not think of a better answer than reading *Enough About Love.*

20. *BOMB* called it "a French intellectual sex romp."

21. *The New York Times* called it the key to unlocking one of life's central questions: "At least as intriguing as how the French

make their bread taste so good is how they manage all those extramarital love affairs they're said to have."

22. "We'll be surprised if it leaves your hands," chirped the style blog *Daily Candy*.

23. An enthusiastic blogger called *The Book Lady* attempted to count the ways in which she loved the book, concluding "I love it for amusing me, for making me think, for providing a window into other lives that helped me see my own more clearly and for being the perfect companion on a quiet afternoon."

24. There is something weird about this kind of reception.

25. Something about *Enough About Love* was communicating at another level.

26. If it were a book written by an American, about Americans, I very much doubt Lorin Stein would have found it "cute."

27. That kind of praise is reserved for books from France.

28. Americans love France, and Americans loathe France, and Americans love to loathe France.

29. How is it that French children don't throw food and their women don't get fat and they don't die of heart attacks and they all have such robust and non-monogamous sex lives? And how did she tie her scarf that way?

30. American readers are prepared, when faced with a mediocre French book, to find some redeeming qualities because it is French, just as they're prepared, when faced with a fluffy self-help book, to hate it more because it is French.

31. The Dalkey books didn't get anywhere near as much press or praise.

32. Michael Orthofer reliably wrote about them in his *Complete Review*, calling them "entertaining," though he wasn't blown away by either.

33. *Publisher's Weekly* wrote of *The Sextine Chapel* that it "seduces the reader with its wry wit" but that "the humor can be limp too."

34. That's a mean thing to say about a penis-driven narrative.

35. (Guess Le Tellier really isn't writing Oulipo 'ard.)

36. *A Thousand Pearls* received barely any reviews, except for a guy called Jeremy on Goodreads.com, who called it "a charming glimpse into the profundity and banality of one man's random thoughts."

37. All four of these books are steaming piles of sexism and masculine privilege.

38. Worse, they're unfunny, clichéd and shot through with narcissism disguised as self-awareness.

39. There is a problem when this kind of writing can find a home on two distinguished publishers' lists.

40. I can think of a few explanations why Dalkey would have published these books.

41. They're taking advantage of the success of *Enough About Love* (the marketing explanation);

42. Any Oulipian text must be worth publishing by virtue of its being by an Oulipian (the co-opted avant-garde explanation);

43. Harry Mathews is on the board and is looking out for his fellow Oulipian (the nepotism explanation).

44. The percentage of books that are translated into English are "overwhelming male-authored," noted Michael Orthofer: "around 80% in 2010."

45. In 2011 that was down to 78%.

46. So being a non-Anglophone male makes you more likely to have your work published in translation in the US.

47. But whatever its language of composition, there's a certain kind of work that gets published for reasons other than its own merit.

48. How else can I put this? Dude books rule.

49. Reading the best literary journals and book blogs, an alien visitor to our *république des lettres* would be forgiven for thinking that our leaders are called Pynchon, DeLillo and

Wallace, and that they are subtended by a group of men named William (Gaddis, Gass & Vollmann).

50. I can't think of a single female author who is as universally imposed on readers by editors and critics.

51. Can you?

52. "It takes the authority of a male voice to write from the center of culture," I once heard the novelist Siri Hustvedt say. "As women, we're just barking from the margins."

53. This is what it sounds like at the center of culture: "After a series of multiplications including centimeters, frequency and various other intimate parameters, Laurent figures out that over the past twenty years his penis has traveled 12.5 kilometers inside a female body" (from *The Sextine Chapel*).

54. This type of manthmatics (manth for short) really grosses me out.

55. I'm not sure Le Tellier would agree with my characterizing him as being at the center of anything; he presents himself as one of those nebbishly fragile-psyched beta-males who just want to be loved (on which, more below), and nebbish beta-males are in the habit of denying their masculine privilege.

56. Le Tellier's female characters are there to be desired and to reject the (male) protagonist. They are sexual objects and rejecting objects. They do not have interior lives and desires of their own.

57. And why would you want to be loved by a sexual/rejecting object?

58. Unless the sexual/rejecting object isn't really the central issue.

59. What is the central issue, then?

60. Oh, that special something Lacan called "lack."

61. By which he meant this: we are born into this world and we linger in a symbiotic harmony with our mothers until that cold hard day when we look in the mirror and understand

that we are ourselves and not an extension of our mothers. We are separate beings.

62. Accepting our subjectivity means we'll always want, and never retrieve, that symbiotic harmony.

63. We are on our own.

64. Refusal to acknowledge or inability to deal with this can lead to a panoply of pathologies, including excessive shopping, co-dependent relationships, and an abuse of social media.

65. Or it can lead to publishing pieces of writing that might be amusing to your friends but really don't stand up on their own merits.

66. In cornering two sectors of the reading public (Francophilic novel-readers and too-cool-for-school experimental fiction-readers) Le Tellier has managed to get himself marketed as someone who can be read and adored by both women and men.

67. This is no mean feat, but perhaps easier for a work in translation, with its whiff of exoticism and difference.

68. Can men get away with more if they are billed as "experimental" writers?

69. Yes.

Oulipo and Sexism

One of the things Oulipians claim sets them apart from other avant-garde groups is that their movement isn't meant to be political. And yet strong Oulipians, like Queneau, Harry Mathews and Perec, have wanted to interrogate the world we live in, largely through a disruptive use of language and a more conscious approach to the everyday world. Queneau's *Zazie in the Metro* (1959) turns the map of Paris inside out; his heroine comes not to see the sights but to see the Metro, and the sights she does see are all scrambled up, one swapped out for another ("Look! The Panthéon!!!" "No, no, and no, isn't the Panthéon.").

Mathews has said that in titling his strange second novel *Tlooth* (1966) he aimed to disturb the very act of reading itself in order to "undermine any...hope of certainty that there may be in reading the text." Perec, for his part, called for his readers to find what is significant in the quotidian: "Question your tea spoons," he exhorted readers of "The Infra-Ordinary." "What's underneath your wallpaper?"

Le Tellier doesn't seem to want anyone to question anything. When he looks in his tea spoons all he sees in them is his own concave, upside-down reflection. Like the Surrealists he tends to see women as ciphers and archetypes—a sexism that's latent in French culture (and avant-garde culture) in general. If Le Tellier were a writer on his own, this would be less important to point out; who has time to keep tabs on every single male chauvinist writer? But the Oulipo is menaced by the reactionary bourgeois element Le Tellier represents. This may be to some extent unavoidable; many avant-garde groups have seen their once-revolutionary ideas appropriated by the mainstream, where they lose their trenchant edge. The Oulipo's loopy experiments have indeed come to seem like reasonable literary experiments. But if the Oulipo hopes to avoid exhausting its potential, it is up to its members to stay outside of the mainstream, writing from the margins rather than from the comfortable center of official culture. If an Oulipian leaves the workbench and settles into a comfortable armchair, his worldview narrows, and his work's potential diminishes.

A vulnerability to sexism was coded into the Oulipo's DNA from the outset.[1] Quick French lesson: an *ouvroir*, Arnaud tells us, "once denoted a shop...in which the master cobblers of Paris displayed their wares and pursued their trade." This title indicates an emphasis on craft, on the made (and potentially anti-realist) quality of a work of literature. It also points up an element of trade associated with an *ouvroir*, where things made to be sold. Until around the eighteenth century *ouvroir* could refer to "that part of a textile factory where the looms are placed; or, in an arsenal, the place where a team of workers performs a given task." In this way the Oulipo identifies itself as a much more grounded endeavor than other manifesto-driven avant-garde groups like the Futurists, the Surrealists, or the Situationists; in the *ouvroir*, we work with our hands, with tools. There is also, it must be pointed out, a distinctly masculine whiff to all of this—master cobblers creating and plying their wares, belonging to guilds, building a network of power founded on male camaraderie.

But *ouvroir* has some other, more feminine connotations. It can refer as well to

a long room where the young women in a community work on projects appropriate to their sex; or a charitable institution for impoverished women and girls who found therein shelter, heat, light and thankless, ill-paid work, the result of which these institutions sold at a discount, thus depriving the isolated workers of their livelihood and leading them (as it was charged) into vice. Later, and for a short time only, *ouvroir* denoted a group of well-to-do women seeking to assuage their consciences in needlework for the poor and in the confection of sumptuous ecclesiastical ornaments.

Built into the term *ouvroir*, then, is a delightful condescension toward women: in the *ouvroir* women do what is "appropriate to their sex"; it is a place where women who have been stripped of any power over their own lives have been sent to be exploited, or a place where overprivileged women can help the poor through the creation of needlework and basically useless ornaments. The potential for women in the ouvroir is restricted.

The Oulipo was founded by a group of men in 1960, though women were eventually admitted: in 1975 Michèle Métail joined, though she has subsequently distanced herself from the group; the poet Michelle Grangaud 20 years later, in 1995; the novelist and scholar Anne Garréta in 2000; the systems analyst

Valérie Beaudoin in 2003; and finally the mathematician Michèle Audin in 2009. (The group seems to have decided, when appointing female members, to employ the constraint that they must be named some variant of Michelle.)

The Oulipians borrow from the last definition of *ouvroir* to claim that they are doing benevolent work, casting themselves in the role of bourgeois women doing needlepoint. According to Queneau, the Oulipo "search[es] for new forms and structures which may be used by writers in any way they see fit," tools which writers can use as handily as a needle, thread and openwork canvas. This is why they protest that they are neither a school, nor a movement. They are a "research group," Jean Queval has explained, adding to our body of knowledge of potential things; they even see themselves as a "nursery school," according to François Caradec.[2] The mixed metaphors would seem to be part of the point—the idea of pre-schoolers engaged in researching the intersection of literature and mathematics being the kind of delightfully surreal image the founding Oulipians loved.

But, like most research groups, the Oulipo is indeed a *métier d'homme*. All that math. All that game-playing. It's hard, as a woman, to know what to make of the Oulipo, or where we might fit in to its project. It's not that girls don't like math: some do (just as some boys don't). Girls also like games. And the idea of creating literature within certain constraints—why, women have been doing that for centuries. (Surely hiding the manuscript of your novel under your needlepoint and writing in jags when no one is looking constitutes an early Oulipian procedure.) Women writers are virtuosos at operating within constrained circumstances. But the Oulipo—particularly Oulipo Lite—can seem slightly juvenile and pointless. Even women who love the Oulipo get impatient with it: "Lots of men sitting around doing crosswords," said one of my experimentally inclined friends in an anti-Oulipo mood.

The Oulipo has already been criticized for being macho. At a conference in 2005, Juliana Spahr and Stephanie Young delivered their Foulipo manifesto, in which they critiqued the "masculinist tendencies of most constraint-based writing" in a tract that adopted some of that constraint-based writing. They wondered if the Oulipo was not "pehaps toubled by an uninvestigated sexism and thus not capable of being a pat of ou witing life in any way, a question we didn't eally want to ask because we wee scaed of the answe and what it would deny us."[3] But does it matter if the Oulipo is a boys' club? What's wrong with a bunch of men sitting around doing anagrams? Why does it matter how many women are members? To what extent does gender really matter for the Oulipo or its readers? What do we want from the Oulipo?

A little dissent, perhaps. A little acknowledgment of their masculine privilege. I don't think women feel alienated by the Oulipo because women are inherently uninterested in games and constraints, but rather, through the work of Oulipians like Le Tellier, back through the long history ofthe avant-garde, women are made to feel as if, time and again, we have no place as subjects and agents of literature; we are only its objects.

Feminism and the Oulipo have more in common than one might think. Like Queneau and Perec, feminists have attempted to read life and literature against the grain. Critics like Rachel Blau Duplessis have argued that all existing poetic forms are fundamentally "male-gendered." Feminist poets must address this formally: "Nothing changes by changing the content only." The Oulipo, however, depends on pre-established (male-gendered) poetic forms like the sonnet and the sestina to provide a basic constraint. Other feminist critics from Barbara Guest to Adrienne Rich have proposed various degrees of rupture; they insist, as Kathleen Fraser writes, "on the primacy of reinventing language structures in order to catch one's own at-oddsness with the presumed superiority of the central mainstream vision."

This is what Spahr and Young were getting at in their manifesto: that the (masculinist) techniques of the Oulipo were considered still to have relevance while the (feminist) body-based arts evolving at approximately the same time are now considered heavy-handed and narcissistic. This was not intended as a critique of constraint itself but rather of what the privileging of Oulipian procedure and the dismissal of body-based arts implied, what was "slenderized"[4] out of the Oulipo and what perceptions were imposed on the naked female body:

We did not feel this wok that uses constaint was ielevant, not to men no to women. We did not want to dismiss it. When we liked this wok by men we saw the eteat into constaint as an attempt by men to avoid pepetuating bougeois privilege, to make fun of the omantic nacissistic tadition, of all that tadition of fomalism. But at othe moments we ween't so sue that this was eally a feminist, antiacist self-investigation. While this wok diectly avoided emotional and pesonal expessiveness, it was mostly engaged with conceptual inventiveness, not an especially adical move post the tun of the centuy.[5]

Whatever one's methods, avant-garde art must stage a continual intervention in the status quo if it is to resist being co-opted, and defused, by the mainstream.

Desire and Decline

The French title of Le Tellier's *The Intervention of a Good Man* (2007) was *Je m'attache très facilement*, a reference to Romain Gary, which in the English version is used as an epigraph ("I get attached very easily"). It's not really clear why the title *The Intervention of a Good Man* was chosen; it doesn't make a lot of sense once you've read the book, and it weighs the novel down with sentiment about the hero's character. By contrast, the French title foregrounds the hero's tendency to get over-invested. For who is more deserving of love than a "good man," as the title urges us to consider our hero? (There is another alternative—a kindly Scotsman—but his intervention is so minor that it cannot truly be the focus of the novel.) One wonders if it is under the heading of this unambitious goodness that he gets away with being a letch.

The Intervention of a Good Man is probably the least Oulipian of Le Tellier's works, but, as Le Tellier has said himself, any work produced by an Oulipian is to a certain extent Oulipian.[6] It was originally published by Les Mille et une nuits, an imprint of Fayard, which specializes in publishing slim, small-format books, about 3 by 5 inches, generally of texts in the public domain. Sounding a little like it was written by the publisher, the Wikipedia entry for Les Mille et une nuits (an Oulipian resource if ever there was) notes that this format makes the books particularly convenient given the "constraints of urban life (commuting, waiting around)" and that the authors published by the imprint are very often "audacious (they have published several anarchists as well as numerous unknown ideologues)." In recent years, Mille et une nuits has expanded its operations to produce books of standard paperback size as well. It is then, like the Oulipo, a publishing house torn between anarchists and classics, between ideology and marketing, between the portability of the small format and the conventionality of the larger one. Where does Le Tellier fit in?

The story is set in Scotland, where "our hero" (as he is referred to, chorally, by the narrator) has come to be with one of those very blond women, one who is 20 years younger than he, and who is "almost" married to someone else. She's just not that into our poor hero, a vain yet somewhat self-aware, aging man, but this just keeps him on the line for her: he desperately needs her to validate him, somehow. Our hero's romantic rival is also

20 years older than this very blond Scotswoman, but our hero does not believe he poses much of a threat.

The threat itself seems to emanate from this unpredictable, un-self-aware young woman, who seduces without "thinking of seducing," and who "seems to think" that the three years she has been with the other man is a "huge" amount of time, though our vain, aging hero knows it is not. It may have been a mistake for our hero to come to Scotland, but he reassures himself with an Oscar Wilde quote that the things we regret are never our mistakes.

We learn less about the Scotswoman herself, although she is the object of the novel. Our hero tells us she is "intelligent and cultivated," but he hasn't been able to find out if she is funny, because he spends so much time attempting to impress *her* with *his* wit. The thing about this girl that keeps our hero interested is—have you guessed it?—she is "pretty, very pretty." And "she knows it, of course." (The hero's musings are liberally peppered with "of courses," to indicate how modestly, sadly, worldly wise he is.) We get a description of what kind of pretty she is: "tall, slender, with delightful little breasts, and her regular cycling keeps her small buttocks firm; her face is dusted with freckles." The description of her bosom rings off-key; to whom is it delightful? To our hero, of course. As for his physique, he is more tanned and slightly more toned than the last time they met (but he has taken care not to look too much better, because he "would still not like to be too different from the man he was when he managed to seduce her"). Hard to imagine the blond Scotswoman finding his body "delightful," but this is the point—the vain, aging hero attempting to seduce the delight-fully breasted younger woman will always feel slightly inade-quate. Cue neuroses-driven non-plot.

Le Tellier's narrator keeps a tight watch not only on his characters but on the way his characters might be interpreted, anticipating the reader's judgments and conceding that, yes, the reader might be right. (He also congratulates himself for deciding to keep a diary of his misadventures—he dares not think in terms of "adventures," which in French refers to love affairs.) The narrative is written in the present tense, to give (one imagines) immediacy to the proceedings and to the hero's now-or-never, I-am-aging need. For this is the central subject of the book: *I am aging, please want me love me need me*. The self-awareness is so pronounced that one wonders if the need to be liked is restricted to the character of the vain aging hero, or if there is not some bleed over into the authorial persona as well.

I will say in Le Tellier's defense that he does not present himself as a writer who has figured it all out; rather he moves over the emotional topographies of his characters as if he were reading Braille. And yet—this is what makes him just so skeevy. He runs his fingers over all of his female characters, trying to figure out what they mean, what they want, who they are. He doesn't mean any harm; he's just trying to love and be loved. What more basic human desire is there? Yet the "love" our hero feels for the young blond Scotswoman is so intermingled with desire that he wonders whether he actually loves her or if he only ("only") desires her.

He reflects on the addiction built into the term "heroine": he is "genuinely dependent" on her. Like a drug, she is there for him to enjoy; she does not possess her own interiority. This is no longer a crime in fiction—E.M. Forster's comparison of round versus flat characters rings old-fashioned. But the love story is simply so hackneyed, so absent of any stakes, except insofar as we may feel somewhat bad for this vain aging hero. The novel announces its own futility at every corner, as if the very novel itself—The Novel, not only this one—could only lust after young women and mope about its own ineffectiveness. But this does not reflect some postmodern crisis of The Novel where love and sex are concerned: it reflects only the limits of Le Tellier's imagination. He wants to write about love, but he also doesn't want to write about it. He wants to write about sex, but can only write about its banality.

Our vain aging hero attempts to put a name to his feelings for the young blond Scotswoman. His need for her is addictive, but is it love? Let's see. "What does he think of when he thinks of her? Her eyes, her mouth, the back of her neck, other parts of her body that no listing could ever exhaust. This is a physical desire, one he could never fight. But what drives him toward her first and foremost is a sense of suffering, which at some points he lucidly analyzes as a fear of losing her.... He does love her—we should not be afraid to use the words—and is aware that he should not." But why should he not love her? Nothing we are explicitly told would seem to endorse this kind of judgment; on the contrary, we seem intended to sympathize with him.

Does she desire him back? (Can a drug want you back?) Signs point to no; much like an inanimate object, "She is quite capable of going for days on end without giving any sign of life." The only sign of anything she gives is in the sack, when he can tell "from the taut feel of her young body beneath his hands that he has been synonymous with pleasure for her, every time they have met." Note the phrasing: he can tell from the feel of her body beneath his hands that she is enjoying herself, but she does not communicate, except inaudibly, tactilely. He "wants her skin to long for his, and to prove it to him every moment."

Perhaps Le Tellier gets stuck in the banality of love and sex because he is trapped at the level of the epidermis. In his books a woman is there for his enjoyment, or she is a terrifying, mysterious creature capable of devouring a man with one snap of her perfectly whitened teeth. This is not a worldview; this is not a philosophy. This is a constraint which the Oulipo should give up.

Put Love in the Title

I will, however, give Le Tellier credit for bringing love into the

Oulipo. Exploring the bonds that link people together in love or lust isn't often a theme in Oulipian novels, or of experimental novels in general; perhaps it should be. Love itself is a kind of constraint. Love imposes form.

But what can the Oulipo bring to a love story?

Le Tellier's 2009 novel *Enough About Love* tries to take an honest look at people in love, and mostly succeeds, hitting a few false notes mainly where the women and their self-images are concerned (but we'll get to that). A set of crisscrossing characters meet, fall in love, uncouple, and recouple: Anna falls for Yves (though she is married to Stan and he is with Ariane) and Louise falls for Thomas (though she is married to Romain). Thomas is Anna's therapist, the kind of well-connected Left Bank Paris shrink who has photographs of himself with Lacan and with Barthes on his shelves. Each chapter shuffles this cast of characters, bringing each one momentarily into contact with another.

Its Oulipian predecessor is without a doubt Harry Mathews' *Cigarettes*, but where Le Tellier's vision of love is exclusively concerned with sleazy older men lusting after younger women, *Cigarettes* looks at all different kinds of love in addition to heterosexual relationships—different kinds of sexual relationships (lesbians, gays, S&M) as well as non-sexual relationships (fathers and daughters, artists and subjects, critics and artists).

As in *The Intervention of a Good Man*, middle-aged masculine insecurities infuse the text. Yves Janvier, a middle-aged writer, worries about what he has achieved in his career to date, taking some solace in the fact that he makes his living from words, though he worries he does not make a comfortable enough living. "You have readers, but you haven't yet found your true readership," his editors assure him. Wooing the married Anna Stein, Yves gives her a copy of his latest book "with the unusual title *The Two-Leaf Clover*." The description of the novel sounds perfectly matches *The Intervention of a Good Man:*

The book, which is very short, relates with ferocious intensity an emotional disaster, a restrained and clinical dissection of a lover's fantasy: a story as old as time itself about an older man who, having become infatuated with a young women and having seduced her a bit, but not enough, decides to go an join her in Ireland — which explains the title — where he collides head-on with her withering indifference in the most magnificent fiasco. The irony with which it is told made her laugh, and she thought: this man's an expert.

With Yves as the author of a book which strongly resembles one Le Tellier himself has written, Yves would seem to be a double for Le Tellier.

Also like Le Tellier, Yves writes novels with constraints. His latest project is a book provisionally titled "Abkhazian Dominos," a variation on the classic game of dominoes played in Abkhazia, a "small former Soviet republic on the Black Sea." Le Tellier first goes into a long-winded discussion of how to play said dominos game before explaining how the novel based on the game will work: there will be six main characters, and each will get his or her own domino, with "the novel will reproduc[ing] the trajectory of a game of Abkhazian dominoes." But — wait! That sounds more or less exactly like the novel we've been reading, with its configurations and re-configurations of characters. In fact, the characters are domino tiles!

Yves wants to call the novel "Abkhazian Dominoes," but doesn't plan to explain its structure to the reader. Le Tellier, of course, has just explained it to the reader. But Yves doesn't stick to his own rules — and neither, one might infer, will Le Tellier. (Yves also doesn't end up keeping the title; Anna quite sensibly tells him to pick something more universally attractive: "Put 'love' in the title," she says.)

The text's awareness of its own status as a text is calculated; Le Tellier can never stop commenting on his own limitations as a writer, but this doesn't come across as a postmodern refusal to boonswaggle the reader with the constructed world of the novel so much as a self-flattering nod at Le Tellier's own self-awareness. "How to describe the beginnings of love?" Yves wonders. "That eternal question. Of course, 'eternal question' is a cliché." This superficial self-awareness, and the strategic use of self-deprecation, is a cover for self-concern.

In this fictional self-portrait, Le Tellier includes a sketch of the writer as fighter, heroically battling clichés ("Yves is a writer because he would not write 'infinite tenderness,' 'life's journey,' or 'hopelessly in love' without feeling ashamed") and "pummel[ing]" easy wording. But what Yves/Le Tellier is really after—that most elusive of literary pursuits—is to represent reality on the page: "His words try to depict real things, like flagstones covering beaten earth: but, in places, rebellious weeds poke through."

It's not clear what these rebellious weeds are meant to represent—are weeds less real than flagstones?—but the lopsided binary provides a nice metaphor for the way Le Tellier's own work attempts to use the synthetic constraints of the Oulipo to get at the real of fiction, while the weeds of sexism keep growing up to disturb (one infers) his work's aesthetics.

Clearly Le Tellier is trying to make the reader question the relationship between the real and the fictional through his description of the constraints at work; however "real" these characters may seem, however beaten and polished the language, it is the work of an Oulipian mastermind. But the weeds—those pesky weeds. No matter how attuned Yves/Le Tellier may try to be to language, mannerisms, pleonasm and rhythm, no matter how dedicated he may be to stomping them out, the weed-clichés about women come poking out of the ground, overwhelming the text to the point of near unreadability.

Enough About Stereotypes

Le Tellier's sexism is truly overt in the case of Anna Stein, one of the four protagonists of *Enough About Love*. Though each protagonist is vain in his or her own way, Anna is the only one whose preoccupation with her appearance is a defining element of who she is. Le Tellier writes her from the outside, never quite able to penetrate what her interest in clothing might mean. We first see her through the eyes of her shrink, Thomas (who is also, in a way, a double for Le Tellier): "Anna Stein's outfit is distinctive, as usual. Wide white pants that fit tightly over her buttocks to define them clearly, a fleetingly transparent, midnight blue blouse, and a shiny, black trench coat." But in the very next phrase, we are meant to leap into Anna's own perspective on her body: "She chooses her clothes carefully, her long tall figure allowing her to wear things that would be fatal on others. She sees herself as slim, lives being slim as synonymous with being rigorous. Gaining weight, she is convinced, is always a lapse."

Something about this description rings false. Maybe it's because it comes not long after a description of Anna as a teenager, her emotional maturation focalized through her body: "At 15, Anna ties her black hair up to reveal the nape of her neck. She triumphantly inhabits her brand-new woman's body: she wears leopard-skin leggings and high heels, aggressive bras." I'm reminded here of Angela Carter's discussion of male writers in drag as female characters, "Lorenzo the Closet Queen," in which she takes D.H. Lawrence to task for his fetishistic attention to women's clothing in *Women in Love*. Calling it "Lawrence's most exuberantly clothed novel," she criticizes Lawrence for using Gudrun and Ursula's clothing to define them as characters. "Details about clothes are just the sort of thing a man would put into a book if he wanted the book to read as though it had been written by a woman," Carter writes. "Lawrence clearly enjoys being a girl." Carter's quoting Oscar Hammerstein II's lyric for "Flower Drum Song," but I'm also reminded of "How Lovely to Be a Woman" from the cultural milestone that is Strouse & Adams's "Bye Bye Birdie":

How lovely to be a woman
the wait was well worthwhile
How lovely to wear mascara
And smile a woman's smile
How lovely to have a figure
That's round instead of flat!
Whenever you hear boys whistle
You're what they're whistling at!

Is this what men think of female puberty? That we suddenly wake up one day, look in the mirror, clasp our newly sprouted breasts and dance around? (Later, Anna describes her breasts as having been "arrogant." I have a hard time picturing a woman describing her breasts in those terms, but I supposed it could happen. There are a lot of different kinds of women around.)

Fast forward to the present moment: "Anna Stein is about to turn 40...Because she thinks there is a before and an after, as commercials for hair products, she is already living in mourning for what has been and in terror of what is yet to come." Of course women worry about aging (as do the men in this book), but in the reference to hair product commercials Le Tellier gets in a real dig at Anna. (Is she perhaps based on a cruel ex-girlfriend?) Certainly unintelligent women can be a subject for fiction—why not? But there is something troubling about the way these analyst-writer-lovers see women.

In *Enough About Love*, Anna's body has a will of its own. Yves writes to her, "I like looking at you naked, you like me looking at you...your buttocks turn and rise up toward me, their every curve wanting to arouse me, their soft, soft skin intended just for me. You smile, and this gesture gets the better of me, I'm gripped by desire, you are mine and I take you." Anna—her volition, her desire—is reduced to her buttocks; they have agency but she can only be "taken."

Louise is Anna's less superficial, more down to earth foil: she has a great sense of humor, references the Oulipo, makes bad puns and can command a room full of lawyers. She teaches her husband how to address a crowd. And yet she is a "little blond slip of a woman." We're meant to think—oh she's so little and yet so powerful! And yet—were she physically threatening it would be too much; the book would sink under the terrifying fixating power of Louise Blum. It is at her most astounding debut performance—giving a speech to win entry to the Paris Bar—that she meets her husband. Just as she moves out of bounds, she is folded back in, defused of her threat by the conformity of marriage.

Louise also exists through her clothes, but they give her a confidence Anna lacks, and this works to solidify her relationships rather than splinter them. When she goes out, she "put[s] on her makeup and this black dress which—she knows for sure—really suits her," and when she goes out "She knows that there are men on cafe terraces looking at her, right now, as she walks up the Boulevard Saint-Germain." She jokes to Thomas that when she goes out, "it's to show off my ass." Thomas smiles with confidence: "In spite of everything, he doesn't actually mind if she shows it off, that ass of hers."

The novel turns marriage into an Oulipian constraint, cleverly following Jacques Roubaud's principle that the constraint must be the theme of the novel. Oulipianly, Le Tellier probes these love affairs, tunneling toward their exhaustion. Le Tellier has the conventions of the love story to get out from under, and the adultery plot is as limited in its outcome as a toss of the dice (or a game of dominos?). What are the possible outcomes? They stay together. They stay together and the partner finds out. They stay together and the partner doesn't find out. They break up and (or because) the partner finds out.

They break up and (even though) the partner doesn't find out. They break up and the partner finds out and the lover becomes the new partner. They break up and the partner doesn't find out and the lover becomes the new partner...Etc, etc, etc. There are more outcomes but it's boring to list them. The point is: two millennia of the love plot have exhausted it. What is the Oulipian writer to do, then, except treat marriage and infidelity like a game?

Yet Le Tellier saps Oulipian procedure of any urgency it might be thought to contain. It's fine to set up the novel like a game; this is part of the novel-writing craft. And this kind of constraint brings the novel closer to poetry, in the sense that its various components (chapters instead of verses) are more strictly formalized. But somehow it robs the characters of their free will, and forces them to do the bidding of an authorial God. If Barthes's now-canonical essay declared the death of the author, Le Tellier's novel reassures us that he's alive and well and living in Paris.

Love and Exhaustion

Banality is the other side of love, its inevitable sequel, and Le Tellier makes it his principle theme. Modernism taught us how to cope with, and even appreciate, literary banality; Proust turns boredom into a narrative device to great effect in *In Search of Lost Time*. In fact, you could argue Proust's use of the banal brings his novels closer to some concrete idea of "the real" precisely because it observes the progression of thought in an average mind. But with Le Tellier, rather than exploring banality from an aesthetic or philosophical perspective you get the distinct impression that he's trying to validate his own banality by attributing it to his characters, by making it the very essence of humanity. In the early sections of *Enough About Love*, when we are learning about Yves' struggles with weeds, we are treated to some of the "incomprehensible notes" contained in Yves's diary:

"Jupiter's moons. Twelve. Some can be seen with the naked eye." and "Being on the crest. Climbing up from the valley to be on the crest. No interest in the mountain per se."

A few pages earlier, Yves Janvier also noted:

"What is it about the rain that I like so much?"

"Why have I always hated having my picture taken?"

"We talk about overwhelmed and underwhelmed, but is anyone ever whelmed?"

"The left cerebral hemisphere controls speech (Paul Broca)."

"Abkhazian dominoes, the only game of dominoes where, if you can't play, you are allowed to pick up a domino that's already on the board."

Placing the banal in a work of literature is a great and noble tradition in French literature going back at least to Flaubert and Balzac. But whereas, in *Species of Spaces* or *W.,* Perec uses the banal in order to get at something larger than himself (war, displacement, abandonment, organic and inorganic change, capitalism) Le Tellier's use of it shows he has a difficult time thinking of anything other than himself and things that directly concern him—like love, sex, rejection, and how bloody boring it all can be. Perec aims to overturn ordinary everyday banality to question its underlying assumptions and values; Le Tellier just wants to quip and get laid.

Le Tellier confronts banality head-on in his epigraph to *The Sextine Chapel* (2005), which comes from Roland Barthes: "Sexual practices are banal, impoverished, doomed to repetition, and this impoverishment is disproportionate to the wonder of pleasure they afford." As Le Tellier narrates one interlude: "Cunnilingus, then fellatio, then penetration, then orgasm (or not)....Terence thinks how right Foucault was: sexuality is quite monotonous." Le Tellier takes up this idea and builds on it, exploring chains of sexual partners in a series of vignettes depicting the coupling (ok, the fucking) of Anna and Ben, Ben and Chloe, Chloe and Dennis, all the way through the alphabet to Yolande and Zach, where it starts again: Zach and Anna, Anna and Harry, Harry and Oriane, etc. Each person appears in six vignettes with six different partners. A table of contents lists all the pages on which you can see each of the characters in action, so to speak.

Think of all the people you've been with, then the people they've been with, and the people they've been with—nothing makes you want to settle down with one sexual partner like a book that shows you all the potential wackos in your sexual group. And because this is a book by an Oulipian, some of those people have been the same people. (The Oulipian allergy to chance and randomness would seem to demand this; Le Tellier is trying to build an erection with a specific set of blueprints; the Oulipianness of the blueprints would seem to call for some limits to be imposed, but, à la *Hundred Thousand Billion Poems*, wouldn't it be far more interesting for Le Tellier to have found a way for his core group of people to be linked up to *Hundred Thousand Billion Lovers?*).

As with *Enough About Love*, Le Tellier owes a debt to Harry Mathews, but here he makes that debt explicit: *The Sextine Chapel* is dedicated to Mathews and proves to be an homage to his *Singular Pleasures* (1983), a collection of 61 short scenes of people around the world wanking off. But *The Sextine Chapel* has none of Mathews' ingenious perversion. Mathews' text spins ever wilder scenarios of people masturbating—alone, together, homosexually, heterosexually, without even touching themselves directly, with tree-trunks, in Gaza, and on the edges of glaciers: "Somewhere north of the Bening Straits, sitting on the edge of an ice floe, his face impassive, all movement concealed beneath thickness of pelt and fur, an Eskimo male of

31 is bringing himself to an orgasm of devastating intensity in a slickness of dissolving blubber." Toward the end of *Singular Pleasures* Mathews suddenly invents a group called MAID, or Masturbation and Its Discontents, whose members invent obstacles to be overcome while they masturbate.

The Oulipian constraints used to build *The Sextine Chapel* are as monotonous as a boring sexual encounter; here's how Le Tellier described *The Sextine Chapel* to *Bookforum*:

I first decided to use three constraints that all relate to the number 78.

First the ceiling: the 26 characters correspond to the letters of the alphabet and each character makes love to six other characters, each scenario unfolding according to a particular circular rotation.

For the floor of the chapel: the number 78 is the sum of the numbers of one to 12, and from this I was able to construct a series of triangles within a larger triangle, with 12 triangles as its base.

Are you still reading? Here's the rest, feel free to skip over it:

Every chapter (a small triangle) contained a[n] element of reference (often well-hidden) to the chapter that surrounds it, another small triangle in the larger triangle.

For the "stairs" that go from floor to ceiling...I used the sextine, a formal poetry of the troubadours, consisting of six stanzas of six verses, and ending with the "envoi," composed of three verses. Or 39 verses in all. In the sextine, the words at the end of the verses of the first strophe (1 2 3 4 5 6) turn like this, for the second strophe (6 1 5 2 4 3), and so on, five times. Two successive sextines equal 78 lines in total.

There are images in the back of the book: the floor of the Sextine

Chapel and the ceiling of the Sextine Chapel. One is a set of triangles showing each page number in a triangular relationship to the others, together forming one big triangle that looks like a checkered floor, except the checks are triangles. And the ceiling is a circle of criss-crossing lines connecting each person to his or her partners, their names listed around the edge of the circle like an astrological chart. If you're not into math you won't care about the illustrations.

In *The Sextine Chapel*, the vignettes are 100% heterosexual, which seems really weird, and some of them are downright orientalizing, as someone called Rémy "finger[s] the delicate hairs of [Qiu's] jade-colored, oriental pubis." Mathews indulges in this kind of exoticization as well, but to such an absurd extent that it's impossible to take seriously. Le Tellier on the other hand casts his couples in bourgeois locations like the Museum of Natural History or behind a formica countertop. He tries to be funny, but it falls flat: "Pierre thinks how much kisses are like pickles in a jar. One you manage to extract the first one, the others come of their own accord."

What Le Tellier was trying to do in *The Sextine Chapel*— which, I assume, is write engagingly and interestingly about uninteresting sexual encounters—has been done more success- fully elsewhere, not only by Mathews but by Nicholson Baker, whose recent porno-novel *House of Holes* is louche, border-trans- gressing, and original. (On this point I disagree with my colleague Barrett Hathcock, who in *Lady Chatterley's Brother* takes Nicholson Baker to task for having in *House of Holes* completely omitted any semblance of character or plot devel- opment. Surely modernism has disabused us of a need for either.)

The confluence of sex and mathematics would seem to indicate that *The Sextine Chapel* wants to legitimize sex as a casual recreational activity akin to driving or skiing, and writing as a sequence of not very interesting observations. It takes the particular talent of an Oulipian to blend mathematical principle with the romance-killing mathematics behind our love affairs. But on the other hand, it may be the too-perfect interior architecture of Le Tellier's texts that turns them into works frozen in their own forms, much like the nineteenth-century novel rejected by the modernists, laden with accumulated detail.

Although Le Tellier told *Bookforum* that the themes are not the same in *Enough About Love* and *The Sextine Chapel* ("*The Sextine Chapel* talks about sex, the sexual act, without love (incidentally, the book does not contain the word *tenderness*), while *Enough About Love* addresses the issue of love and desire"), I think he means to do more than just be funny, and the book's delightfully heretical take on the Sistine Chapel seems to support this. The book is a massive orgy of people groping each other—the title of the book, one imagines, referring to the animating touch from God's finger to Adam's in Michelangelo's ceiling. Through touch, we are given life. Following this logic, Le Tellier's characters grunt and strain and rut in a frantic group attempt to fuck themselves into life. And yet, life eludes them: they are characters stuck in a book by an author who has already decided that their pursuits are banal and their women destined to disappoint them. *The Sextine Chapel* represents a philosophical unseriousness toward a serious philosophical problem. Faced with the pointlessness of it all, Le Tellier seizes on the female body as a source of validation, but it provides only disappointment at every turn.

How Would You Like Your Oulipo?

Le Tellier has written an impressive treatise on the subject of the Oulipian aesthetic; this aesthetic, if it can be said to exist, has to do with the pleasure that the reader takes in deciphering the text—*le plaisir du texte*.[7] This may consist of recognizing the constraints, "but not necessarily." Defining the aesthetic in this way, Le Tellier suggests, "eliminates any illusion that we can analyze the quality of a work, allows subjectivity to enter the aesthetic judgment and imposes the term 'complicity.'"

Oulipian reading calls for a different kind of engagement with a text—it has to do with a heightened awareness with what else the language may be saying apart from what it seems to be saying. In some cases, as in *The Intervention of a Good Man*, the Oulipian reader may look for constraints in vain. (Even if the author has said there aren't any constraints, the reader may ask, how do we know for sure?) It "differs from regular reading only in the reader's degree of complicity with the author," writes Daniel Levin Becker. "There's a different kind of attention that the Oulipian texts calls for, inherited from modernism, which calls on the reader to move from passive receiver of the text to active collaborator/decipherer of its meaning." So whether or not the Oulipian writer has advertised his (or her) constraints, it is still a question "of making you, the reader, aware of your own effort and engagement, of putting you in control, of diminishing the distance between finding and making."

The difference between Oulipo Lite and Oulipo 'ard may have to do with this complicity between reader and writer. Is the reader just hanging out listening to funny poems punctuated by ringing bells? Or is the reader working with the text, figuring out its constraints, its meaning. But this dichotomy would seem to separate Oulipian culture into "high" and "low," and there's room for all variants of Oulipo at the table. Being entertained with word games is as valid a way of spending an evening with an Oulipian as pondering the absence of *e* in Perec's *A Void*. But Le Tellier's Oulipo Lite violates the complicity between reader and writer through a reactionary approach to sex and gender. I wince when a literary double for a writer writes of a younger female's "pretty young body beneath his...the nape of her neck docile to his kisses." I mean, gross. It's no wonder his "good man" keeps striking out with women—he traps them in exteriority.

Oulipo is about what's inside. It explores the silent spaces between letters and words, investigating language to reveal latent meanings. There is nothing inherently sexist or macho in this pursuit. The Oulipo will be fine if it can shed this chauvinist inheritance, and if it can learn instead to promote members like Anne Garréta, who in her novel *Sphinx* (1986) eliminates all references to her two main characters' genders. (This was one of the reasons she was invited to join the group, according to Jacques Roubaud in an interview with *BOMB Magazine.*) Garréta's prose is elegant and even mannered, without being prim. *Sphinx* is a very intense book; it is *déchirant*, it rips itself to shreds. Composing a love story without revealing if the narrator and the central love interest are men or women is a neat device, particularly difficult to achieve in French because so much of the language reflects the gender of the speaker and the addressee; but Garréta manages, in line with Roubaud's principle, to make the constraint the subject of the novel. Bodies are repeatedly hidden throughout the course of events, just as, through grammatical evasion, Garréta hides the sex of her lovers from the reader. She gives us images of looking without deciphering — the stare of the deceased, who see without seeing; the throng of bodies in a dance club, monstrous in their undefinability but somehow prolonging their lives through their togetherness; the image of the narrator's body as s/he stares at him/herself in the mirror, stepping out of the shower. We are shown only his/her wrinkles, his/her fatigue, the outfit s/he decides to wear; we see nothing specific, for the novel tells us that specificity not only doesn't matter but is somehow impossible. The very nature of love and being is at odds with a deciphering gaze. Understanding carries with it a finality that Garréta attempts to keep at bay.

This translates as well into a superstition of linear narrative. The narrator can't render her love "discursive" when s/he wants to declare it to his/her lover, who is called A*** in the text:

I alternated (and received no response) between snatches of stories and accounts of my interior monologues, between syllogisms and images, moving without transition from slang to an elevated style and from the trivial to the abstract without ever finding the right ton or appropriate genre in which to make my speech.

A postmodern narrative that is very much of its time, *Sphinx* points a way for literature to escape the confines of fictional narrative. Garréta's constraint answers the challenge of feminist critics to "reinvent language structures"—or at least avoid certain structures—"in order to catch one's own at-oddsness with the presumed superiority of the central mainstream vision." The elimination of gender in a love story might prove an interesting Oulipian exercise for Le Tellier to undertake.

Garréta's work is wide-ranging and provocative; Dalkey or Other would do well to publish her in English. McSweeney's published her wonderful piece "On Bookshelves" in 2007; why not a translation of her novels from their publishing arm? Why should the Oulipo continue to be a *métier d'homme*—why not allow for it to become a *métier de femme*?

Why not indeed?

Notes

1. Daniel Levin Becker describes the evolution of the group from Queneau's day to our own as a change "from an environment where a bunch of gentlemen sat around discussing Literature to one where a bunch of dudes sat around talking lipogrammatically for the sport of it" (208).

2. François Caradec: "The Oulipo is not a school; it's a nursery where we force cylinders into square holes and cubes into round ones while our parents and proctors aren't looking. Does it work? Depends on the day" (in Levin Becker, 7n1).

3. When Spahr and Young gave the manifesto as a talk at the Noulipo conference at Cal Arts in 2005, they did so while taking off their clothing and putting it back on a couple of times, and at a certain point in their talk their voices were replaced with a recording of themselves speaking. A friend who attended said that when they were finished, "shit broke down, there was a lot of yelling and accusations and the final reception was canceled because no one would be in the same room with each other."

4. Slenderizing is removing all instances of a letter from a text, turning it into a lipogram.

5. As I was writing the above 69 theses, I thought of Foulipo and wondered why it is that to make a feminist critique of the Oulipo we have to do it in Oulipian terms. Are we feminists so afraid of being dismissed that we have to play by the rules of the very thing we're critiquing? Or are we — to take a well-worn phrase from the heyday of feminist literary criticism — adopting those constraints *to subvert them from within*? There is one letter missing from my 69 (aha!) theses. Does it matter? It certainly doesn't turn it into a great Oulipian work.

6. Of course, Harry Mathews has said the exact opposite.

7. Le Tellier does strike me a serious guy, one who has thought seriously about the Oulipo, its history, and its operations. Which is why, in spite of the foregoing, I believe there is hope for him.

A By No Means Exhaustive Potential History of the Oulipo, in the Form of a Timeline

1960 — Oulipo founded as the Séminaire de littérature expéri-mentale. Name formally amended to Ouvroir de littérature potentielle at the group's second meeting.

1961 — First Manifesto.

1965 — Publication of *The Blue Flowers* by Raymond Queneau.

1967 — Jacques Roubaud becomes first co-opted member of the Oulipo.

1967 — George Perec joins the Oulipo.

1969 — Publication of *A Void* by Georges Perec.

1973 — Second Manifesto.

1973 — Italo Calvino joins the Oulipo.

1973 — Harry Mathews becomes the first American member of the Oulipo.

1973 — Publication of *La Littérature potentielle*, a collection of representative Oulipian work, brings the group its first broad exposure.

1975 — Publication of *The Sinking of the Odradek Stadium* by Harry Mathews.

1976 — Death of Oulipo co-founder Raymond Queneau.

1976 — The Oulipo hosts its first annual summer workshop, at a Carthusian monastery in Villeneuve-lès-Avignon in the south of France.

1978 — Publication of *Life A User's Manual* by Georges Perec.

1978 — Jacques Roubaud abandons his book *The Great Fire of London*, leading him to begin his masterwork, a seven-book project called *"the great fire of London."*

1979 — Publication of *If on a Winter's Night a Traveler* by Italo Calvino.

1982 — Death of Georges Perec.

1984 — Death of François Le Lionnais, co-founder and president of the Oulipo. Succeeded by Noël Arnaud.

1984 — Julio Cortázar dies in Paris after repeatedly declining invitations to join the Oulipo.

1985 — Death of Italo Calvino.

1986 — Anne Garréta publishes *Sphinx* (Grasset), a novel which tells the love story of two characters whose genders are unclear (a difficult feat in the highly gendered French language).

1986 — Warren Motte publishes *Oulipo: A Primer of Potential Literature*.

1986 — Marcel Bénabou publishes *Why I Have Not Written Any of My Books*.

1987 — Publication of *Cigarettes* by Harry Mathews.

1990 — Founding member Jean Queval dies.

1990 — OuCuiPo (Workshop of Potential Cuisine) is founded.

1991 — OuTraPo (Workshop of Potential Tragicomedy) is founded.

1992 — Jacques Roubaud publishes "Le voyage d'hier" ("Yesterday's Journey"), which builds on and transform's Perec's "Le voyage d'hiver" ("The Winter Journey").

1992 — Hervé Le Tellier conscripted into the group.

1992 — Oskar Pastior joins the group (its first and only Romanian).

1992 — Pierre Rosenstiehl joins the group.

1992 — OuBaPo (Workshop of Potential Comic Books) is founded.

1993 — Jacques Jouet publishes *Le chant d'amour grand-singe* (The Great-Ape Love-Song), a series of poems composed in a language from the Tarzan series called Great-Ape.

1993 — OuHisPo (Workshop of Potential History) is founded.

1995 — Bernard Cerquiligni juins the group after publishing

L'Accent du souvenir, an autobiography of the circumflex.

1995 — Michelle Grangaud joins the group, partly on the basis of her poetry collection *Stations* (1990), composed entirely of anagrams created from the names of Parisian metro stops.

1995 — OuPhoPo (Workshop for Potential Photography) is founded.

1996 — Beginning of the Thursday readings.

1996 — Jacques Jouet composes his metro poems.

1997 — OuCiPo (Workshop of Potential Cinema) is founded.

1998 — Publication of the *Oulipo Compendium* by Harry Mathews and Alastair Brotchie.

1998 — Ian Monk is elected to the Oulipo.

2000 — Olivier Salon is elected to the Oulipo.

2000 — Anne Garréta is elected to the Oulipo: born in 1962, she is the first Oulipian to be younger than the group itself.

2001 — The *Magazine Littéraire* devotes its May issue to the Oulipo.

2001 — OuGraPo (Workshop for Potential Graphic Design) is founded.

2001 — André Blavier, elected to the group in 1961, dies. The group's "foreign correspondent," he lived in Belgium.

2001 — Death of founding member Jacques Bens.

2001 — OuArchPo (Workshop of Potential Architecture) is founded.

2001 — OuPolPo (Workshop of Potential Politics) is founded.

2001 — Michelle Métail tries to leave the group and requests that her name be replaced on the roster with an ellipsis. (Her request was refused.)

2002 — A rival OuGraPo (Workshop for Potential Grammar) is founded.

2002 — Death of founding member Claude Berge.

2003 — The systems analyst Valérie Baudoin is elected to the group.

2003 — OuMuPo (Workshop of Potential Music).

2003 — Noël Arnaud dies. Paul Fournel is elected president, leaving his position of "definitively provisory secretary" to Marcel Bénabou, who adds it to his prior position of "provisionally definitive secretary."

2005 — Death of Jean Lescure.

2005 — Frédéric Forte joins the group after publishing *Opéras-Minute*.

2005 — Oulipo symposium is held at Princeton University.

2005 — nOulipo conference is held at Stanford University.

2006 — Death of Oskar Pastior.

2006 — McSweeney's publishes *The State of Constraint: New Work by Oulipo*.

2009 — Hervé Le Tellier publishes *Esthétique de l'Oulipo*.

2007 — Harry Mathews is interviewed in *The Paris Review's* The Art of Fiction series.

2007 — Ian Monk publishes *Plouk Town*, which Daniel Levin Becker calls "the most significant work the Oulipo has produced since the mid-1990s"

2008 — Death of François Caradec.

2009 — Daniel Levin Becker, the second American and youngest Oulipian, joins the group.

2009 — Michèle Audin joins the group.

2009 — The Oulipo pretty much takes over the first installment of the literary festival Paris en Toutes Lettres.

2013 — OuFrancoPo (Workshop of Potential James Franco) is founded.

2014 — Tom McCarthy joins the group.

2014 — Hervé Le Tellier, helped by Anne Garréta, Michelle Grangaud, Valérie Baudoin and Michèle Audin, writes a feminist manifesto.

2014 — After several false starts, OuPornPo is founded.

2015 — OuBrekPo (Workshop of Potential Breakfasts) is founded.

2015 — Jacques Roubaud wins the Nobel Prize for Literature.

2016 — Oulipo opens for Penn & Teller.

2017 — Christian Bök realizes a longstanding dream by eliciting the spontaneous creation of poetry from inorganic matter.

2020 — After much inquiry and consternation, computational assistance from Google allows the discovery of the hidden *e* in *A Void*.

2025 — Original, subsequently authenticated copy of *The Winter Journey*, publication date 1852, turns up in an Argentine book store.

Further Reading

This list of further reading is not meant to be exhaustive. It is a collection of suggested and beloved books that are currecntly available in English, compiled by two people who have found a lot to enjoy in the Oulipo.

The list is broken down into four groupings: 1) "Prelipo," writers and/or books who anticipated the founding of Oulipo in 1960, or books written before their authors joined Oulipo; 2) "Oulipo," books that come from within the ranks of the group; 3) "Oulipo+," books from writers who never joined the group but worked (or are working) in a distinctly Oulipian mode; and 4) On Oulipo, a straightforward list of helpful secondary sources on the group.

Publisher and year of publication is given for the first edition of each book and the translation, where applicable. In most cases these books are in print and readily available, often in fantastic translations.

Prelipo

Italo Calvino, *Cosmicomics* (1965), trans. William Weaver. Harcourt Brace Jovanovich, 1968.

Italo Calvino, *Invisible Cities* (1972), trans. William Weaver. Harcourt Brace Jovanovich, 1978.

Harry Mathews, *The Conversions* (1962). Dalkey Archive Press, 1997.

Raymond Queneau, *Exercises in Style* (1947), trans. Barbara Wright. New Directions, 1981.

Raymond Roussel, *Impressions of Africa* (1910), trans. Mark Polizzotti. Dalkey Archive Press, 2011.

Raymond Roussel, Locus Solus (1914), trans. Rupert Copeland Cunningham. University of California, 1970.

Oulipo

Italo Calvino, *If on a Winter's Night a Traveler*, trans. William Weaver. Harcourt Brace Jovanovich, 1982.

Harry Mathews, *The Sinking of The Odradek Stadium* (1975). Dalkey Archive Press, 2000.

Harry Mathews, *Cigarettes* (1987). Dalkey Archive Press, 1998.

Harry Mathews, *My Life in CIA: A Chronicle of 1973*. Dalkey Archive Press, 2005.

Georges Perec, *Things and A Man Asleep*, (1965/1967), trans. Andrew Leak. David R Godine, 2010.

Georges Perec, *Species of Spaces and Other Pieces* (1974), trans. John Sturrock. Penguin Classics, 2008.

Georges Perec, *Life A User's Manual* (1978), trans. David Bellos. David R Godine, 2008.

Jacques Roubaud, *The Loop* (1993), trans. Jeff Fort. Dalkey Archive, 2009.

Jacques Roubaud, *Mathematics* (1996), trans. Ian Monk. Dalkey Archive, 2012.

Oulipo+

César Aira, *Ghosts* (1990), trans. Chris Andrews. New Directions, 2009.

César Aira, *The Literary Conference* (1999), trans. Katherine Silver. New Directions, 2010.

César Aira, *An Episode in the Life of a Landscape Painter* (2000), trans. Chris Andrews. New Directions, 2006.

Joe Brainard, *I Remember* (1970). Granary Books, 2001.

Christian Bök, *Crystallography*. Coach House Books, 1994.

Christian Bök, *Eunoia*. Coach House Books, 2001.

Julio Cortázar, *Hopsctoch* (1963), trans. Gregory Rabassa. Pantheon, 1987.

Edouard Levé, *Autoportrait* (2005), trans. Lorin Stein. Dalkey Archive, 2012.

Edouard Levé, *Suicide* (2008), trans. Jan Steyn. Dalkey Archive,

2011.

Matt Madden, *99 Ways to Tell a Story: Exercises in Style.* Chamberlain Bros, 2005.

Michael Martone, *The Blue Guide to Indiana.* Fiction Collective 2, 2001.

Tom McCarthy, *Remainder.* Vintage, 2007.

Vladimir Nabokov, *Pale Fire* (1962). Lancer Books, 1989.

Lance Olsen, *Head in Flames.* Chiasmus Press, 2009.

Padgett Powell, *The Interrogative Mood: A Novel?* Ecco, 2009.

Gilbert Sorrentino, *Mulligan Stew* (1979). Dalkey Archive, 1996.

On Oulipo

David Bellos, *Georges Perec, A Life in Words.* David R. Godine, 1993.

Daniel Levin Becker, *Many Subtle Channels: In Praise of Potential Literature.* Harvard University Press, 2012.

Peter Cosenstein, *Literary Memory, Consciousness, and the Group Oulipo.* Rodopi, 2002.

Harry Mathews & Alistair Brotchie, eds. *Oulipo Compendium.* Atlas, 1998; repr. Make Now Press, 2005.

Warren Motte, *Oulipo: A Primer of Potential Literature.* Dalkey Archive Press, 1998.

Contemporary culture has eliminated both the concept of the public and the figure of the intellectual. Former public spaces – both physical and cultural – are now either derelict or colonized by advertising. A cretinous anti-intellectualism presides, cheerled by expensively educated hacks in the pay of multinational corporations who reassure their bored readers that there is no need to rouse themselves from their interpassive stupor. The informal censorship internalized and propagated by the cultural workers of late capitalism generates a banal conformity that the propaganda chiefs of Stalinism could only ever have dreamt of imposing. Zer0 Books knows that another kind of discourse – intellectual without being academic, popular without being populist – is not only possible: it is already flourishing, in the regions beyond the striplit malls of so-called mass media and the neurotically bureaucratic halls of the academy. Zer0 is committed to the idea of publishing as a making public of the intellectual. It is convinced that in the unthinking, blandly consensual culture in which we live, critical and engaged theoretical reflection is more important than ever before.